THE GOURMET
TOASTER OVEN

THE GOURMET
TOASTER OVEN

Simple and Sophisticated Meals for the Busy Cook

Lynn Alley

Photography by Joyce Oudkerk Pool

TEN SPEED PRESS
Berkeley | Toronto

To M—with love…as always

Ten Speed Press
Box 7123
Berkeley, California 94707
www.tenspeed.com

Distributed in Australia by Simon and Schuster
Australia, in Canada by Ten Speed Press Canada, in
New Zealand by Southern Publishers Group, in South
Africa by Real Books, and in the United Kingdom and
Europe by Airlift Book Company.

Cover and text design by Catherine Jacobes Design
Food styling by Andrea Lucich
Food styling assistance by Lorraine Battle

Library of Congress Cataloging-in-Publication Data
Alley, Lynn.
   The gourmet toaster oven: simple and sophisticated
meals for the busy cook / Lynn Alley.
     p. cm.
Includes index.
   ISBN-10: 1-58008-659-4
   ISBN-13: 978-1-58008-659-2
  1. Toaster oven cookery. I. Title.
TX840.T63A44 2005
641.5'89—dc22   2005048619

Printed in China
First printing, 2005
1 2 3 4 5 6 7 8 9 10 - 09 08 07 06 05

CONTENTS

ACKNOWLEDGMENTS

To the gang at Ten Speed Press, the most author-friendly publishing house I know. Thanks to Phil Wood and Lorena Jones for once again believing in me and one of my projects. Thanks to Carrie Rodrigues for a great and patient editing job. Thanks to Mark Anderson and Dennis Hayes for selling it, to Kristin Bryan Casemore for publicizing it, and never let me forget Kristine Standley for paying me!

To my mom, Margaret Zink, who fortuitously "fried" my conventional oven, leaving me with no means of baking potatoes or bread and thus initiated the hunt for the perfect toaster oven.

And once again, to my eager neighbors, who are always willing to stop by for something new: Helen Mildner, Marie Pike, Rosella Heffner, and Bob, Ernest, and Paul Tassoni.

To Lad and Crystal, my best buds, ever present in my home and always loving me unconditionally, whether in the loping, slobbering way of dogs or the elegant, arrogant, detached way of cats.

To those purveyors who generously supplied equipment and technical information and backup: Catherine Bourdais from Staub USA, Karen Kazam and Judy Mora at DeLonghi, Le Creuset, Tufty Ceramics, Krups, Black and Decker, and Cuisinart.

Many years ago, while I was in college, I rented a room in a beautiful old house in Berkeley. Stephen Felgar, a quiet, scholarly astronomy student, rented the room next to mine.

In the days before running had become fashionable, Felgar would run a good six miles every afternoon. When he returned home from his run, he'd slather up a piece of white bread with a thick coating of peanut butter and toast it until bubbly in his toaster oven. No one ever saw Felgar eat anything but "hot peanut butter sandwiches."

Like Felgar, most of us have a pretty limited repertoire of toaster oven dishes. We melt cheese on toast or English muffins, heat tortillas, and occasionally heat up a TV dinner or a Hot Pocket.

But for me, all of that changed when my mother picked me up at the airport one day and announced that she had accidentally turned the microwave on for fifteen minutes with nothing in it, thinking she had turned on the timer. As a result, the floor and door of the microwave had melted, turned black, and begun smoking. Since the microwave and the oven were in one piece, I knew the whole bundle would have to be taken out and trashed.

Within a week of my return, the old microwave and stove had been pulled out of the kitchen and a gaping hole remained where they once stood.

Mom and I went shopping together, and after weeks of looking, I finally lost my heart to a Jenn-Air Pro-Style downdraft, dual-fuel, top-of-the-line range with a grill on top. I had visions of grilling freshly made pitas or naan, veggies from the garden, and anything else that would not splatter grease all over my shiny new range. Unfortunately, the dealer didn't have one in stock, so the stove's ETA would be at least three more weeks down the road.

Sure, I had a battery of slow cookers left over from research on my last cookbook, but you can't bake good bread in a slow cooker. I had wanted to get a new toaster oven for a long time, and this seemed like the perfect opportunity to do it.

(My former toaster oven, a good one but decrepit with age, had recently dropped its door on my foot.) So, with scientific fervor, I read up on the subject and went comparison shopping for a toaster oven that would meet my needs.

I also began to wonder if it might be possible to take a toaster oven, like a slow cooker, uptown. From toast to, say, Savory Cheesecakes with Artisan Whole Wheat–Walnut Loaf. Or Baked Eggs. Or maybe a replica of my favorite Café Fanny granola.

And just as I set about answering these questions and wondering if such a book might appeal to the gourmet reader, Sam Gugino, the *Wine Spectator*'s food columnist, ran a column about the comparative merits of toaster ovens—an act that in my mind officially elevated the toaster oven from the realm of the lonely-pensioner-in-a-tiny-apartment or the bachelor-who-lives-on-toasted-peanut-butter-sandwiches to the affluent, upscale there's-only-one-or-two-of-us-in-the-kitchen-and-we're-busy crowd. Of course, there's also the sophisticated-college-student crowd, the gourmets-on-the-yacht, the cabin-by-the-lake crowd, and the happy singles (whether retired or working), and let us not forget the growing number of owners of upscale RVs who might want to venture into the gourmet realm with this handy little device. The toaster oven, like the slow cooker, is perfect for numerous small venues.

What's so useful about a toaster oven? Here are some of the reasons why toaster ovens make good sense:

* They take up less space.

* They preheat quickly (5 minutes or less).

* They cook small quantities more efficiently.

* They use anywhere from $1/2$ to $2/3$ the energy a conventional oven uses.

* They're generally easy to clean.

* They're cheaper than conventional ovens.

* They won't heat up the whole kitchen or house on a hot day.

* They may include rotisserie or dehydrating attachments.

* Most have a large window allowing for a clear view of the oven's contents.

* They're portable.

* Some models can be suspended underneath the kitchen cabinets.

In contrast to old-style toaster ovens, whose primary job was to toast bread, melt cheese on English muffins, or heat up TV dinners, modern toaster ovens offer a larger capacity, convection baking, and even rotisserie attachments. In addition, most modern toaster ovens maintain cooler exterior surfaces and are a cinch to clean.

What you'll find in this book are some of the fruits of my foray into the world of the toaster oven. These are dishes I like to eat and that I think real people like to eat. In most cases, the number of ingredients and the work involved are minimal, but the results should be something you'll be proud to serve and happy to eat.

Here are some unique ideas for making the most of your toaster oven.

* You can make a huge batch of cookie dough, then put individual scoops on a cookie sheet as if you were going to bake them, but freeze them instead. Once they are frozen, toss them in a freezer-weight plastic bag to keep in your freezer. Then, any time you want fresh cookies, just pull out one or two at a time to bake and eat them hot out of the toaster oven. (See the Tea and Goodies chapter.)

* You can make half a dozen muffins, eat one or two, and then freeze the rest to heat up one at a time for subsequent breakfasts. (See the Breakfast chapter.)

* You can make a large batch of basic dough, form it into rounds, and freeze them. This way you will always have dough on hand to easily make pizzas, calzones, samosas, or piroshki. (See the Lunch chapter.)

* You can make a big batch of raw ingredients for granola (nuts, oats, seeds, raisins, vanilla, spices, or whatever), and then bake up a cup or two at a time for a breakfast of warm, fragrant, freshly baked granola. (See the Breakfast chapter.)

＊ You can prepare an incredible side dish or appetizer in your toaster oven when you are entertaining to free up your main oven for the entrée or dessert.

With a little careful planning, you should be able to come up with meals that are sophisticated but that can save you time and effort when you're in a hurry or when you'd rather put your feet up and relax than fuss around in the kitchen.

Testing the Recipes

All of the recipes in this book were tested in a convection toaster oven using the convection setting. Does this mean that if you own a toaster oven without a convection setting that you can't use it? Of course not. In many cases, the time and even the temperature settings will remain the same. In some cases, a simple adjustment of temperature will make the difference. (In general, cookbooks recommend that convection baking temperatures be 25°F lower than in a conventional oven. I'm not sure this is an accurate assessment of the situation, but I recommend that you experiment.) Be aware that even if you are using a convection toaster oven, models vary from manufacturer to manufacturer and even model to model, so you still may need to experiment to get to know your oven well.

I have collected a set of baking pans that I use again and again in the toaster oven. Whenever possible, I suggest a certain pan and, at times, even a manufacturer. You may not have the exact size pan I recommend in each recipe. If you are using a different size pan, you may need to alter the ingredient amounts or baking times to suit the pan you are using.

If possible, purchase a large capacity toaster oven. Although the small ones may be less expensive, you may find that you cannot bake bread or muffins in them as there is not enough room to allow the dough to rise. Some of the recipes in this book may not be appropriate for smaller ovens.

Price

As with most anything else in life, you get what you pay for when buying a toaster oven. The pull to pick up that $29.99 toaster oven on sale at the local department store may be strong, but chances are the amount of pleasure, use, and convenience you'll get out of it won't be worth the money you will save by not buying a quality piece of merchandise.

Be smart. Do some comparison shopping. Toaster ovens I have tried and enjoyed are the higher-end models made by Cuisinart, DeLonghi, Black & Decker (Dining-In series), and Krups. All are priced above $100, but all are a pleasure to work with, and each has special features to recommend it. The Black & Decker, for instance, has a 14-inch interior, while the others have a 12-inch capacity oven. The newest DeLonghi convection toaster oven is deep enough to accommodate a 12-inch pizza.

Basic functions: Grill, broil, toast, and convection bake. Convection baking is essentially baking that relies upon a fan for even heat distribution. It may result in more even cooking, and it may also hasten cooking times.

Removable crumb tray: Nearly all toaster ovens today are made with a removable crumb tray to make cleaning easier. No more turning the toaster upside down and shaking it onto the counter.

Timer: Wouldn't it be great to have a toaster oven that turned itself off after 15 minutes (or whenever)? Some do, and some don't. Be sure to check.

Nonstick interior: This is another feature almost always found in better toaster ovens that saves a lot of scrubbing. If you follow my suggestions about a good once-a-week cleaning, your toaster oven should last a good long time.

Cool-touch exterior: Ensures that you won't burn yourself on the oven while it's on by keeping the exterior of the oven relatively cool. This is an especially good feature if you have kids in the house, although I don't recommend turning your kids loose on the toaster oven unattended, whether it has a cool-touch exterior or not.

Good warranty: Most toaster ovens offer a one- to three-year warranty. The longer, the better. Be sure to check.

Customer service and tech support: This could be important. Although chances are you will never have to use it, wouldn't it be nice to know you could pick up the phone and get your questions answered quickly, courteously, and accurately? Some companies have very poor customer support, while others are just terrific. Make sure a customer service number is included with your toaster oven.

Cleaning Your Oven

Keep your toaster oven impeccably clean from the get-go.

We've all known people (mentioning no names) who have a dirty little toaster oven stashed in a corner somewhere. No one wants to eat food made in a dirty little toaster oven. Keeping your oven clean from the start makes cleaning less of a chore. It will make your food taste better and your oven last longer. The following are a few tips for keeping your toaster oven clean:

* Always unplug your toaster oven before cleaning it. Take out the rack and crumb tray and give it a thorough weekly cleaning. If you do this regularly, you will not have to think about it and your oven will stay new much longer.

* Use one of those small round brushes used for cleaning espresso machines to brush crumbs out of hard-to-reach places.

* Clean interior surfaces with a nonstick finish with mild detergent or according to the manufacturer's instructions.

* Nothing works like pure, cheap rubbing alcohol to cut grease. When the oven is completely cool, pour a bit of alcohol on a sponge and wipe or scrub all surfaces of the oven (except the nonstick ones), both inside and out. Then, with a clean, damp sponge thoroughly wipe off the alcohol. (Be sure to check your manufacturer's instructions first, as they may have their own ideas about what you should use to clean your oven. Their instructions, of course, should supersede mine.)

* Wipe down the interior of the roof of your oven after each use. The hardest place to clean is the interior roof of the oven. Because it usually does not have the same nonstick finish as the rest of the interior, grease accumulates on it easily.

* If your manufacturer allows it, cover the crumb tray and baking tray of your toaster oven with aluminum foil to help save time and effort when cleaning up. However, some manufacturers, such as Cuisinart, caution against the use of aluminum foil in the toaster oven, so be sure to check your manufacturer's instructions before using foil, whether to cover foods or the baking tray.

Potholders

I use thick cotton gardening gloves as toaster oven potholders. They allow for greater movement of the hands than potholders or heavy oven mitts do, and I find they offer enough padding for me to get things quickly in and out of the oven. Make sure to buy a pair that contain no rubber or plastic and have a nice, thick, fuzzy lining.

Always use great care when cooking with cast-iron utensils, which I recommend in a few places, because they get very hot. These are best handled with heavy oven mitts or pot holders.

Oven Rack Positions

Some brands of toaster oven have only one oven rack position; others have several. Pay attention to your chosen brand and place the oven racks in the optimal position for the job you want to do.

Bakeware

As I mention in several places in this book, one way to elevate toaster oven dishes from the mundane to the exceptional is to choose baking and serving dishes that are attractive or unique in some way.

Some of my favorite pans are Staub enameled cast-iron cookware. I love their sleek design and unique nonstick finish. These pans are weighty, distribute heat evenly, and give a beautiful crust to all sorts of foods. I use the 6- and $7^1/_2$-inch round roasting dishes all the time.

Alfred Bakeware's beautiful terra-cotta-colored earthen baking dishes, in particular their loaf pans, are wonderful to bake with. They give a beautiful crust to breads and cakes. I've gotten the most use out of their regular and mini-loaf pans, the small quiche dish, the pie pan, and the 12-inch au gratin dish. All make attractive table presentations.

Le Creuset's custard dishes (for both desserts and individual meatloaves) and their bright yellow au gratin dish also get a lot of use in my kitchen.

WINE SUGGESTIONS

Five years ago, the idea of suggesting wines to go with foods prepared in a toaster oven would have been viewed as a ridiculous proposition.

But things have changed. Today the toaster oven is still the tool of choice for toasting bread and making open-faced sandwiches, but with so many of us devoted to good eating and convenience, the toaster oven is finding a place in the home of the gourmet diner. What formerly produced foods fit only for pairing with a can of diet cola or beer may now be turning out perfectly cooked steaks to go with a good old Bordeaux or a Napa Valley cab.

As with all wine and food pairing, open-mindedness and a willingness to experiment are key. I have made some suggestions for wines to go with the dishes in this book, but they should by no means limit your choices.

BREAKFAST

Breakfast is a meal I never skip. No matter how rushed I am, a nice, simple breakfast seems an excellent way of introducing good things into my day. A well-prepared cup of tea in a fine china cup or earthenware mug with a simple baked egg and a piece of toasted homemade bread or with a small cup of homemade granola topped with fresh, thick yogurt, honey, and fruit will hold me over for hours.

The toaster oven is a great option for preparing breakfast. Toaster ovens pre-heat quickly, and they make enjoying a warm meal at the beginning of the day—when we are often rushing—attainable.

The ingredients for most of these recipes can be prepared the night before. I often, for instance, place a large mixing bowl with all the dry ingredients for a muffin or bread recipe on the counter at night. Then in the morning, all I need to do is to mix in eggs and milk. As an additional time-saver, I freeze any leftover muffins or slices of bread and pull them out in the morning, heat them in my toaster oven, and eat them on the go.

Basic Whole Wheat Bread

MAKES 1 LARGE OR 2 SMALL LOAVES

Nothing could be more simple than using a food processor and a toaster oven to turn out a great loaf of bread. The food processor does all the work of kneading the dough in a matter of minutes. Be sure your oven is large enough to accommodate not only the bread pan of your choice, but also an extra two or three inches of head space for the bread to rise. You can freeze this dough for up to three months to use at a later time. ✳ *I make this bread using freshly ground whole wheat flour, which I mill at home just prior to baking. The texture, flavor, and aroma are grainy and nutty. Use store-bought whole wheat flour if you do not own a home grain mill. This bread makes an excellent toast, filled with vitamins, minerals, and fiber.* ✳ *Finding creative places for your dough to rise is fun: In your car on a sunny day while running errands? Inside the dishwasher after you've just used it? Wrapped in a down jacket or quilt? In a warm, sunny window? A slice of this bread, lightly toasted, with peanut butter or a thin slice of cheese constitutes my favorite early morning breakfast.*

Place the flour, gluten, and salt in the bowl of the food processor. Pulse the food processor several times in order to blend the ingredients.

Place the yeast, honey, buttermilk, butter, and warm water in a glass measuring cup or bowl and allow the mixture to stand for 10 minutes. (To ensure that your bread will rise, it is always a good idea to proof the yeast to make sure it is viable before proceeding. If the yeast is viable, bubbles will form on the surface. If they have not formed after 10 minutes, discard the ingredients and repeat the step with fresh yeast.)

3 cups whole wheat flour (see note)

1 tablespoon gluten

1 teaspoon salt

1 package ($2^1/_4$ teaspoons) yeast

2 tablespoons honey

$^1/_4$ cup buttermilk

2 tablespoons melted butter or oil

$1^1/_4$ cups warm water

Turn the food processor on and, with the machine running, pour the yeast mixture through the feed tube. The dough is ready when it forms a ball in the processor and cleans the sides of the bowl.

Generously brush the inside of a large bowl with oil and place the dough in the bowl. Cover the bowl with a damp tea towel and allow the dough to rise in a warm spot for about 1¹/₂ hours, until it has doubled in size.

If you do not have a food processor, place the flour in a pile on a wooden work surface. Sprinkle the salt, gluten, and yeast over the top of the pile. With your fingers form a hollow in the middle of the pile and pour the buttermilk, honey, and oil into it. Gradually add the water into the hollow, a few tablespoons at a time, mixing it in with your fingers or a fork. Always incorporate the water from the *inside* of the hollow, so that it doesn't leak through and cause water to run all over your counter. The dough will begin to hold its shape, and you will begin to knead the flour rather than mix it. (The amount of water you will need may vary according to the type of flour you are using.) Knead the dough until it is smooth, shiny, and no longer sticky. Place it in an oiled bowl, cover it with a damp tea towel, and let it rise for 1 to 2 hours, until it has doubled in bulk.

Brush 1 large or 2 small loaf pans with oil.

After the dough has risen, punch it down and shape it into either 1 large loaf or 2 small loaves, and then place the dough into the prepared pan or pans.

Spray a piece of plastic wrap with oil and place it over the dough. Allow the dough to rise for another 20 to 30 minutes.

About 5 minutes before the dough has finished rising, preheat your toaster oven to 350°F.

Brush the tops of the loaves with buttermilk and carefully slash them diagonally with a serrated knife.

Bake the bread until it is golden brown (the loaf should sound hollow when thumped on its bottom), about 25 minutes if you are baking 2 small loaves, or 35 to 40 minutes if you are making 1 large loaf.

Remove the bread from the toaster oven and allow it to cool before removing the bread from the loaf pan.

Slice and eat plain or toasted. The best way to keep the bread fresh is to slice it and store any leftover bread in a plastic storage bag in the freezer.

continued

Bacon Bread

12 strips bacon, well cooked,
well drained, and coarsely
chopped

*Note: This recipe has been tested using store-bought flour, but when I am baking at home, I often like to mill my own grain just before baking, because it makes an incredible difference in the aroma, texture, and flavor of the final dish.

Although milling your own grain may sound daunting, it isn't. Simply pour a cup of wheat, rye, oats, or whatever in the hopper of a home grain mill and out will come a bit more than a cup of freshly milled flour.

To make bacon bread: After the dough has risen the first time, knead the bacon pieces into the dough. Proceed with the recipe. This makes excellent toast for breakfast, as well as bread for a unique kind of BLT: just add garden fresh tomato slices and lettuce.

Basic Breakfast Bread

MAKES 1 LOAF

This dough can form the basis for all sorts of imaginative breakfast breads. The oil, egg, and butter-milk give it a richness that makes it suitable for sandwiches as well as for festive occasions and break-fast (a festive occasion in my book). I've included a few of my favorite variations just to give you some ideas of what interesting directions you can take the basic recipe. I recommend making this versatile dough in a food processor because the processor makes a quick job of the kneading.

Place the flour, yeast, and salt in the bowl of a food processor.

In a glass measuring cup, mix the buttermilk, egg, butter, and honey.

Turn the food processor on and, with the machine running, pour the buttermilk mixture through the feed tube. Let the machine run until the dough forms a ball. The dough is ready when it forms a ball in the processor and cleans the sides of the bowl.

Generously brush the inside of a large bowl with oil and place the dough in the bowl. Cover the bowl with a damp tea towel and allow the dough to rise in a warm place until it has doubled in size, about 1½ hours.

If you do not have a food processor, place the flour in a pile on a wooden work surface. Sprinkle the salt and yeast over the top of the pile. With your fingers form a hollow in the middle of the pile and pour the honey and oil into it. In a glass measuring cup, whisk the egg and buttermilk. Gradually add the buttermilk mixture into the hollow, a few tablespoons at a time, mixing it in with your fingers or a fork. The dough will begin to hold its shape, and you will begin to

continued

3 cups all-purpose flour

1 package (2¼ teaspoons) yeast

1 teaspoon salt

1 cup buttermilk

1 egg

4 tablespoons melted butter or oil

¼ cup honey

knead the flour, rather than mix it. Knead the dough until it is smooth, shiny, and no longer sticky. Place it in an oiled bowl, cover it with a damp tea towel or plastic wrap, and let it rise for 1 to 2 hours, until it has doubled in bulk.

Brush a standard loaf pan with oil and lightly flour a work surface. Turn the dough out onto the prepared surface, squeeze out the air, form it into a loaf, and place it in the prepared pan.

Place the loaf in a warm spot to rise. Spray a piece of plastic wrap with cooking oil and place it on top of the loaf to cover. Let the dough rise again for about 30 minutes, until the loaf has almost doubled in size.

About 5 minutes before the bread has fully risen, preheat the toaster oven to 325°F.

Remove the plastic wrap and place the loaf in the toaster oven. Bake for about 35 minutes, until the top is golden brown. Allow the pan to cool before removing the bread.

Slice and eat plain or toasted. The best way to keep the bread fresh is to slice it and store any leftover bread in a plastic storage bag in the freezer.

To make Lemon Breakfast Braid: In a small bowl, mix the 3 tablespoons sugar, lemon zest, and raisins. When you mix in the buttermilk mixture, add these ingredients to the dough.

After the dough has risen the first time, divide it into 3 strands and braid them. For easy clean-up, cover the toaster oven baking tray with aluminum foil, then place the braided strand on top. (Check your manufacturer's instructions, however, for any cautions against the use of aluminum foil in your toaster oven.) Spray a large piece of plastic wrap with cooking oil and place it on top of the braid to cover. Allow the dough to rise for about 30 minutes in a warm spot, or until it has risen by about half again its size.

Lemon Breakfast Braid

3 tablespoons sugar

Zest of 2 lemons

1/2 cup golden raisins

Glaze

1 cup powdered sugar

3 tablespoons freshly squeezed lemon juice

Fresh rosemary needles and blossoms, for garnish

Strips of lemon zest, for garnish

About 5 minutes before the bread has fully risen, pre-heat the toaster oven to 350°F.

Remove the plastic wrap and place the loaf in the toaster oven. Bake for about 40 minutes, until golden brown. Remove from the toaster oven and allow to cool on the tray.

To prepare the glaze, mix the powdered sugar with the lemon juice. Allow the loaf to cool for about 30 minutes, then drizzle the glaze over the top of the loaf. Sprinkle with fresh rosemary needles and blossoms and strips of lemon zest.

When completely cool, slice and serve.

To make raisin walnut loaf: **Combine the sugar, currants, cinnamon, and walnuts in a small bowl. After the dough has risen the first time, knead the ingredients into the dough thoroughly and proceed as directed.**

To make herbed sandwich bread: **Knead the herbs into the dough after you have removed the dough from the food processor and then proceed as directed. Rosemary is always delicious, but thyme or oregano or a combination of all three also works well.**

Raisin Walnut Loaf

$1/4$ cup sugar

1 cup currants or raisins

2 teaspoons cinnamon

$1/2$ cup coarsely chopped walnuts

Herbed Sandwich Bread

$1/4$ cup of any chopped fresh herb (such as rosemary, thyme, or oregano)

Oatmeal Breakfast Bread

MAKES 1 LARGE OR 2 SMALL LOAVES

This recipe is relatively easy, yet the bread is moist and flavorful. It is excellent when toasted or hot right out of the oven. The oats give added texture and flavor.

Place the flour, oats, salt, and yeast in the bowl of a food processor. Pulse until mixed.

Mix the honey and butter with the buttermilk in a small bowl. With the food processor running, slowly pour the mixture through the feed tube. Continue processing the ingredients until the dough forms a ball.

Remove the dough and knead in the raisins and walnuts by hand. Form into a smooth ball.

Generously brush the inside of a large bowl with oil and place the dough in the bowl. Cover the bowl with a tea towel or plastic wrap and set in a warm place to rise until the dough has doubled in size, about 1 hour.

Brush 1 large or 2 small loaf pans with oil.

After the dough has risen, punch it down and shape it into either 1 large loaf or 2 small loaves, and then place the dough into the prepared pan or pans. Spray a piece of plastic wrap with oil and place it over the dough. Allow the dough to rise for another 30 minutes, until the dough rises just over the top of the pan.

About 5 minutes before the bread has finished rising, preheat the toaster oven to 350°F.

2 cups bread flour

1 cup rolled oats

1 teaspoon salt

1 package (2 1/4 teaspoons) yeast

2 tablespoons honey

2 tablespoons melted butter or oil

1 1/4 cups buttermilk

1/3 cup golden raisins or other dried fruit, coarsely chopped

1/2 cup walnuts, coarsely chopped

Bake until the top of the bread is golden brown, 20 to 25 minutes for the large loaf, or 15 minutes for the small loaves.

To test for doneness, remove the loaf from the pan and knock on the side or bottom of the loaf. It should sound hollow.

Slice and eat plain or toasted. The best way to keep the bread fresh is to store any leftover bread, sliced, in a plastic storage bag in the freezer.

Banana-Walnut Muffins

MAKES 6 MUFFINS

My friend Susan Johnson's garden was a constantly changing work of art, but her cooking, in contrast, was strangely less than desirable—and the brunt of many jokes among her eight children. Her banana-walnut muffins were the exception to the rule. Like both Susan and her garden, they are full of good surprises. ✳ *Each time I bake muffins, I eat one or two hot out of the oven, then freeze the rest as soon as they are cool. Then I cut them in half and toast them as I need them.*

Preheat the toaster oven to 350°F. Brush a 6-muffin tin with oil.

Using a whisk or spoon, combine the flour, sugar, baking soda, and salt in a large bowl. In another bowl, whisk together the egg, oil, buttermilk, and bananas. Add the banana mixture to the dry ingredients and mix just until thoroughly blended. Add the walnuts and mix in. Evenly distribute the batter in the prepared tin.

Bake for about 20 minutes, until a toothpick inserted in the middle of one of the muffins comes out clean. Remove from the oven. Allow to cool for just a couple of minutes, then remove them from the muffin tin and serve while warm.

✳ Note: To give your muffins more texture and a nice banana flavor and aroma, use bananas that are still in fairly good shape, with just a few brown spots on them, rather than old, blackened bananas. Your muffins will turn out better.

1 1/2 cups all-purpose flour

1/3 cup sugar

1 1/2 teaspoons baking soda

1/4 teaspoon salt

1 egg

1/4 cup walnut or safflower oil

1/2 cup buttermilk

2 ripe bananas, coarsely mashed

1 cup coarsely chopped walnuts

Coffee Cake Muffins

MAKES 6 MUFFINS

Who doesn't love coffee cake? These coffee cake muffins, with their delicious, crumbly topping, make great breakfast food as well as a morning or afternoon snack with coffee, tea, or even milk.

Preheat the toaster oven to 350°F. Brush a 6-muffin tin with oil.

To make the muffins, in a large bowl, whisk together the flour, baking soda, and baking powder thoroughly.

In a smaller bowl, whisk together the oil, brown sugar, egg, buttermilk, and vanilla thoroughly.

Add the liquid mixture to the flour mixture and beat together thoroughly. Evenly distribute the batter in the prepared tin.

To make the topping, mix the chopped walnuts, the brown sugar, and cinnamon thoroughly in a small bowl. Sprinkle some of the mixture on top of each muffin.

Bake for about 15 minutes, until a toothpick inserted in the middle of one of the muffins comes out clean. Remove from the oven. Allow to cool for just a couple of minutes, then remove them from the muffin tin and serve while warm.

Muffins

$1^1/_2$ cups all-purpose flour

$^1/_2$ teaspoon baking soda

$1^1/_2$ teaspoons baking powder

$^1/_4$ cup oil or melted butter

$^1/_2$ cup brown sugar

1 egg

1 cup buttermilk

1 teaspoon vanilla or maple extract

Topping

$^1/_2$ cup finely chopped walnuts

$^1/_2$ cup brown sugar

1 teaspoon cinnamon

Bacon and Cheddar Cheese Breakfast Muffins

MAKES 6 MUFFINS

I always try to make something special for breakfast when I have houseguests, and this is one of my favorites. This simple touch—and the smell of bacon cooking—always makes guests feel welcome.

....

Preheat the toaster oven to 350°F. Brush a 6-muffin tin with oil.

Thoroughly mix the flour, baking powder, baking soda, and salt in a large bowl. Add the bacon pieces and the cheese and mix in thoroughly.

Whisk the egg, oil, and buttermilk together in a small bowl, then stir them into the dry ingredients.

Evenly distribute the batter in the prepared tin and bake for about 15 minutes, until a toothpick inserted in the middle of one of the muffins comes out clean. Remove from the oven. Allow to cool for just a couple of minutes, then remove them from the muffin tin and serve while warm.

$1\frac{1}{2}$ cups all-purpose flour

2 teaspoons baking powder

$\frac{1}{2}$ teaspoon baking soda

$\frac{1}{2}$ teaspoon salt

6 slices bacon, well cooked, drained, and coarsely chopped

1 cup grated very sharp cheddar cheese

1 egg

2 tablespoons oil

1 cup buttermilk

Proper Scones

Those heavy blobs of dough that pass as scones in coffee shops across the country are known as "rock scones" in England, a name that seems quite appropriate to me. I prefer the lighter, flakier, proper English tea scone. ✳ *The less you handle this dough, the lighter your scones will be; you only want to mix the ingredients, not knead them. As with muffins, freeze any you don't eat and reheat them in your toaster oven.*

Preheat the toaster oven to 400°F.

In the bowl of a food processor, combine the flour, salt, baking soda, cream of tartar, and sugar. Pulse to blend.

Add the cold butter. Turn the machine on and let run until the butter is just blended in and the dough is the consistency of coarse cornmeal.

Turn the machine off, add the buttermilk and currants, and pulse just long enough to blend the ingredients. Remove the dough from the processor and knead it, using just a few turns to bring the dough together.

Lightly flour a cutting board. Roll the dough out on the floured surface until it is about 1 inch thick. Cut out the scones using a 3-inch biscuit cutter.

Line the toaster oven baking tray with parchment paper. Place the scones on the tray and bake for 10 to 12 minutes, until they are golden brown.

Remove the scones from the oven. Wait as long as you can stand, then split the scones open, slather with apricot preserves, and eat.

2 cups all-purpose flour

1/2 teaspoon salt

1 teaspoon baking soda

1 teaspoon cream of tartar

1 tablespoon sugar

1/2 cup (1 stick) cold butter, cut into 8 pieces

3/4 cup buttermilk, plus additional for brushing

2 tablespoons currants or raisins

Apricot preserves or lemon curd, for serving

Granola

MAKES ABOUT 2 (¹/₂-CUP) PORTIONS

I love granola served either as a cereal with nonfat milk and sliced fresh strawberries or as a topping for thick, creamy yogurt with fresh fruit. I keep the raw ingredients in the freezer so they stay fresh. It takes about 10 minutes to bake the granola to a toasty brown and another 30 minutes for it to become crispy. (It will be soft when you remove it from the toaster oven, but it will crisp up as it cools.) You can reduce the amount of oil and honey in the recipe for fewer calories; you just won't get quite the same crunch. You can also multiply this recipe and store it in the freezer.

Preheat the toaster oven to 325°F.

Thoroughly mix all the ingredients together in a large bowl so that the oil and honey are evenly distributed.

Cover the toaster oven baking tray with aluminum foil and spread the granola mixture on top. (Check your manufacturer's instructions, however, for any cautions against the use of aluminum foil in your toaster oven.) Bake for 10 minutes, or until lightly browned. Stir occasionally for even browning.

Allow the granola to cool before serving. Serve in bowls with organic milk and fresh strawberries or bananas.

¹/₂ cup rolled oats

2 tablespoons honey or maple syrup

2 tablespoons nut, sunflower, or safflower oil

1 tablespoon sunflower seeds

1 tablespoon sliced almonds

1 tablespoon sesame seeds

1 teaspoon vanilla or maple extract

¹/₄ teaspoon ground cinnamon

1 tablespoon raisins or other dried fruit (optional)

1 tablespoon shredded coconut (optional)

Organic milk, for serving

Strawberries or bananas, sliced, for serving

Huevos Rancheros

SERVES 1

I always keep a container of cooked black or pinto beans in my refrigerator, ready to use in tacos, tostadas, burritos, and soups. One of my favorite ways to use them is to make this quick, delicious breakfast. This nutritious dish is cheaper, healthier, and tastier than what you can get at the local drive-through.

Preheat the toaster oven to 350°F.

Place the tortilla on the toaster oven baking tray or in a shallow gratin pan that fits in your toaster oven.

Spread the beans over the tortilla.

Using the back of a spoon, make a hollow in the center of the beans. Crack the egg into it.

Bake for about 15 minutes, until the egg is set to your liking.

Remove the tostada from the toaster oven, transfer it to a plate, and top it with cheese, salsa, avocado, and sour cream and serve.

1 whole-wheat tortilla

1/4 cup cooked black or pinto beans

1 egg

2 tablespoons grated sharp or smoked cheddar cheese

2 tablespoons fresh salsa

2 or 3 slices avocado

1 tablespoon sour cream or Greek yogurt

Baked Eggs

SERVES 2

Baked eggs work well not only for breakfast, but also for lunch or dinner. You will need 2 ovenproof custard cups for this recipe. For breakfast, eat them right out of the cup with a spoon or invert the custard cups, pop out the eggs, and place them atop a nest of hash browns or toast. For dinner, you can let them cool, then pop them out and place them on a salad of fresh greens and croutons.

Preheat the toaster oven to 300°F. Spray 2 custard cups with cooking spray or brush with olive oil.

Crack an egg into each cup and place the cup in the toaster oven for 15 minutes, or until the eggs are opaque white. (You can adjust the time depending on how you like your eggs.)

Remove the eggs from the oven and let them sit, covered with a dish or tea towel, for about 5 minutes to allow them to settle.

Sprinkle the eggs with the herbs, season with salt and pepper, and serve the eggs in the cup. Or, allow them to cool and then pop them out of their cups and serve them on hash browns. (If you have oiled the cups, this should be easy to do.)

The eggs can also be made ahead of time, popped out of their cups, and stored for a few hours in the refrigerator to serve with lunch or dinner salads, either cold or at room temperature.

Nonstick cooking spray or olive oil

2 eggs

1/2 teaspoon chopped fresh parsley or rosemary

Salt and freshly ground black pepper

Hash Browns

One of the benefits of cooking in cast iron is that you can preheat the pan and get a nice brown crust as a result. Staub, a French firm, manufactures some beautifully designed cast-iron cookware (see Resources, page 118). Their 7½-inch round roasting dish is perfect for making hash browns. One caution: always be sure to handle cast iron using thick potholders.

Pour the oil into a cast-iron pan or other roasting dish that fits in your toaster oven. Place the pan in the toaster oven and preheat the oven with the pan in it to 400°F.

Using your hands or a fork, thoroughly mix the potato, ham, and herbs and season to taste with salt and pepper.

When the toaster oven has reached 400°F, carefully remove the pan using thick potholders and set it on a wooden cutting board or folded dish towel.

Carefully spread the potato mixture evenly into the hot pan.

Cover tightly with aluminum foil. (This step is optional. Your potatoes will stay moister this way, but they will cook just as well uncovered. Check your manufacturer's instructions for any cautions against the use of aluminum foil in your toaster oven.)

Bake for 20 minutes, until the potatoes are soft, then remove the pan from the oven. Invert the pan onto a plate to release the hash browns. Cut the hash browns in half and serve while hot.

1 tablespoon olive oil

1 large potato, peeled and grated

Small slice of ham or bacon, finely diced (optional)

1 tablespoon chopped fresh parsley, tarragon, or chives (or a combination of all three)

Salt and freshly ground black pepper

LUNCH

Just about every cuisine in the world features some kind of portable snack: Cornish pasties, Indian samosas, Italian pizzas and calzones, Latin American empanadas, and Russian piroshki—all consist of some delicious filling encased in or sitting atop bread. All can easily be frozen and baked on demand in a toaster oven for snacks, appetizers, or quick meals. Or you can just freeze the dough and wrap it around leftovers or traditional fillings when needed.

In this chapter, I've attempted to simplify things by offering one basic dough recipe that can be used in a number of different recipes. This way you can make up a batch of dough, form it into rounds, then freeze it to use later to make quick pizzas or stuffed breads.

The differences among these dishes are usually found in the filling and sometimes in the method of cooking or the type of shortening used in the dough, but they all follow the same basic pattern. Although traditional Indian samosas are likely to have butter or ghee in them, I use olive oil for health and convenience reasons. Purists may want to consult ethnic cookbooks for truly authentic dough recipes.

Traditionally, calzones and piroshki are formed by placing some filling on half of a round of dough, then folding the other half on top to seal in the filling. Samosas, on the other hand, are traditionally formed by cutting a round in half, making a cone out of each half, filling them, and then pinching the ends to seal. Use whichever method is easiest for you.

Any of the samosas, piroshki, or calzones can be fully made ahead, frozen, and reheated on demand. (Appetizer-size items can be reheated at 325°F for about 10 to 15 minutes, while entrée-size items may take longer, about 20 to 25 minutes.

In addition to the stuffed breads and pizzas, I've included a good sandwich loaf recipe from my friend and master bread baker, Beth Hensperger. You can use this bread with the Cajun Meatloaf (page 49) to make an excellent sandwich, or use it to make the Open-Faced Turkey, Brie, Gouda, and Sun-Dried Tomato Sandwich (page 54).

Enjoy!

Basic Dough

MAKES 4 (8-INCH) ROUNDS OR 6 (4-INCH) ROUNDS

Here is a basic dough recipe that can be used to produce pizzas or various types of stuffed bread. You can easily make a batch or two, roll the dough out into 8-inch rounds, and then freeze them to use later when you want a fresh, hot pizza, samosas, calzones, or piroshki. Or you can make a batch or two of dough to prepare several of each dish and then freeze the unbaked portions to keep quick, freshly baked lunch options on hand.

Combine the salt, yeast, and flours in the bowl of a food processor. With the machine running, slowly pour the water and oil through the feed tube.

Continue running the machine until the dough forms a ball in the food processor.

Generously brush the inside of a large bowl with oil and place the dough in the bowl. Cover the bowl with a damp tea towel and allow the dough to rise in a warm place until it has doubled in size, about 1^1/$_2$ hours.

If you do not have a food processor, place the flours in a pile on a wooden work surface. Sprinkle the salt and yeast over the top of the pile. With your fingers form a hollow in the middle of the pile and pour the oil into it. Gradually add the water into the hollow, a few tablespoons at a time, mixing it in with your fingers or a fork. Always incorporate the water from the *inside* of the hollow, so that it doesn't leak through and cause water to run all over your counter. The dough will begin to hold its shape, and you will begin to knead the flour rather than mix it. (The amount of water you

2 teaspoons salt

1 package (2^1/$_4$ teaspoons) yeast

1 cup whole wheat flour

2 cups all-purpose flour

1^1/$_4$ cups warm water

3 tablespoons olive oil

continued

will need may vary according to the type of flour you are using.) Knead the dough until it is smooth, shiny, and no longer sticky. Place it in an oiled bowl, cover it with a damp tea towel or plastic wrap, and let it rise for 1 to 2 hours, until it has doubled in bulk.

Punch the dough down and then divide it into 4 equal pieces. Shape each piece into a disc, then roll each disc out into an 8-inch round. Alternatively, you can divide the dough into 6 pieces for appetizer-sized pieces.

At this point, you can either stack the rounds, placing pieces of plastic wrap or waxed paper between them, and freeze them in a large freezer bag, or you can use the rounds to make one of the recipes that follow. They thaw easily in 5 to 10 minutes when you are ready to use them.

Chicken and Basil Calzone

SERVES 1

If you were to top half a pizza with your favorite fillings, then fold the other half on top of the filling and press the edges together, you would end up with a calzone—the Italian version of a Hot Pocket. This calzone contains a chicken and cheese filling, but artichoke hearts, Gorgonzola cheese, pesto, pine nuts, prosciutto, or bacon are other possibilities. Cut it in half and serve with a green salad, or keep it whole and eat it on the run.

Preheat the toaster oven to 400°F.

Place the dough round on your toaster oven baking tray. Arrange the slices of chicken on half of the round and spread the ricotta, mozzarella, and tomato sauce evenly over the meat. Sprinkle the fresh basil over the top.

Fold the other half of the round over the top of the filling and seal the edges with either a fork or your fingers. Brush the top of the calzone with olive oil.

Bake for about 15 minutes, until golden brown on top. Allow to cool for 10 minutes before serving.

1 (8-inch) dough round from the Basic Dough recipe (page 35), thawed

3 thin slices chicken breast or ham

1 tablespoon ricotta cheese

1 tablespoon grated mozzarella cheese

2 tablespoons tomato sauce

2 basil leaves, cut in chiffonade

1 teaspoon olive oil or egg white, for brushing

Four-Cheese Pizza

Cheese pizza is a favorite of most American pizza lovers. Here is one that is as delicious as it is simple to make. Feel free to vary the cheeses to suit your taste. I have suggested one of my favorite cheese combinations, but you can easily change the cheeses to suit your personal taste. As far as I am concerned, just about any carefully made cheese is a good cheese.

Preheat the toaster oven to 450°F for at least 10 minutes.

Place the dough round on your toaster oven baking tray, then spread the tomato sauce over the round. Sprinkle the cheeses and garlic over the sauce.

Bake for about 8 minutes, until the crust is golden brown and the cheese is melted.

Sprinkle the pizza with the fresh basil. Allow it to cool for a few minutes, then cut it into quarters, transfer to a plate, and serve.

1 (8-inch) dough round from the Basic Dough recipe (page 35), thawed

2 tablespoons tomato sauce

1 tablespoon grated sharp cheddar cheese

1 tablespoon grated smoked Gouda cheese

1 tablespoon goat cheese

1 tablespoon grated Parmesan cheese

1 clove garlic, finely minced

1 large fresh basil leaf, cut in chiffonade

Mediterranean-Style Pizza

SERVES 1 TO 2

This pizza could just as easily be found in Provence or Athens as in Naples. The ingredients are classic staples of the Mediterranean: cheese, olives, and tomatoes. You could substitute some fresh basil for the oregano if you prefer.

Preheat the toaster oven to 450°F for at least 10 minutes.

Place the dough round on the toaster oven baking tray and spread the marinara sauce over the dough. Sprinkle the feta cheese, garlic, and olives over the top of the pizza.

Bake for about 8 minutes, until the crust is golden brown.

Sprinkle the pizza with the oregano. Allow it to cool for a few minutes, then cut it into quarters, transfer to a plate, and serve.

1 (8-inch) dough round from the Basic Dough recipe (page 35), thawed

2 tablespoons marinara or Bolognese sauce

2 tablespoons crumbled feta cheese

1 clove garlic, finely minced

2 to 3 kalamata olives, chopped

Leaves from 1 sprig fresh oregano, chopped

Mexican Pizza

SERVES 1 TO 2

This simple pizza combines with some flavors commonly found in Mexican dishes: tomatillos, cheese, cilantro, and shrimp. Feel free to add or subtract ingredients as you see fit. You use either canned or homemade tomatillo sauce, as time permits.

Preheat the toaster oven to 450°F for at least 10 minutes.

Brush the toaster oven baking tray with oil. Place the dough round on the tray and spread the tomatillo sauce over the dough. Place the tomato slices on top. Dot with the goat cheese and shrimp, and sprinkle the Monterey Jack on top.

Bake for about 8 minutes, until the cheese is bubbly.

Sprinkle the pizza with fresh cilantro. Allow it to cool for a few minutes, then cut it into quarters, transfer to a plate, and serve.

1 (8-inch) dough round from the Basic Dough recipe (page 35), thawed

2 tablespoons tomatillo or green chile sauce (canned or fresh)

1 small tomato, thinly sliced

2 tablespoons goat cheese

1 or 2 fresh shrimp, uncooked, peeled, and deveined

1 tablespoon grated Monterey Jack cheese

1 tablespoon chopped fresh cilantro

1 lime, sliced, for serving

Piroshki

SERVES 4

Piroshki, also known as pirogi, perogi, piroghi, perogy, *or* pirozhki, *are the Russian and Eastern European equivalent of a savory turnover. They are usually filled with typical cold-climate ingredients such as potatoes, ground meat, mushrooms, cabbage, or a combination of any of these. Seasonings, if any, are usually simple: salt, pepper, caraway, or fresh dill, and they are often served as an accompaniment to soup with a dollop of sour cream.*

Preheat the toaster oven to 400°F.

To make 4 meal-size piroshkis, roll out 4 dough rounds on a lightly floured work surface.

Place about $1/3$ to $1/2$ cup of the filling on half of each round, then fold the other half over the top. Crimp the edges with a fork to seal. Using a pastry brush, brush the piroshki with egg white.

Place the piroshki on the toaster oven baking tray and bake for about 20 minutes, until they are golden brown. Allow to cool for a few minutes, transfer to a plate, and serve.

To make appetizer-size piroshki, roll out the dough rounds on a lightly floured board, then, using a 3-inch cookie or biscuit cutter, cut about 6 or 7 rounds from each round. Brush each round with a bit of egg white, place a scant tablespoon of the filling on half of each round, and then fold the other half over the top of each. Crimp the edges with a fork to seal. Using a pastry brush, brush egg white over the top of each piroshki. Bake the piroshki on a toaster oven baking tray for about 15 minutes, until they are golden brown. Allow to cool for a few minutes, transfer to a serving tray, and serve.

1 Basic Dough recipe (page 35), thawed

1 filling recipe from page 43

Egg white, for brushing

To make the meat filling, brown the meat and onion in a frying pan over medium-high heat, about 10 minutes, then add the dill and season with salt and pepper. Stir in the hard-boiled egg. Remove from the heat and add the sour cream to the meat mixture just before filling the piroshki. Proceed with either the meal- or appetizer-size piroshki instructions above.

To make the mushroom filling, heat the butter in a frying pan over medium heat. Add the mushrooms and sauté for about 10 minutes, until lightly browned. Remove from the heat and add the hard-boiled egg and just enough sour cream to moisten the mixture. Proceed with either the meal- or appetizer-size piroshki instructions above.

To make the potato and cabbage filling, heat the butter in a frying pan over medium heat. Add the potatoes, onion, caraway seeds, and cabbage and sauté for about 10 minutes, until browned. Remove the vegetables from the heat and add the sour cream to moisten the mixture. Proceed with either the meal- or appetizer-size piroshki instructions above.

Meat Filling

1 1/2 pounds lean ground beef

1 onion, chopped

1 teaspoon finely chopped fresh dill

Salt and freshly ground black pepper

1 hard boiled egg, finely chopped

1 tablespoon sour cream

Mushroom Filling

1 to 2 tablespoons unsalted butter

1 pound fresh mushrooms, cleaned and chopped

1 hard boiled egg, chopped

1 to 2 tablespoons sour cream

Potato and Cabbage Filling

1 tablespoon unsalted butter

1 large potato, boiled, peeled, and cut into 1/2-inch cubes

1/2 onion, chopped

1 teaspoon caraway seeds

1 cup chopped cabbage

3 tablespoons sour cream

Samosas

SERVES 4

Samosas are a very popular Indian snack food. They are most commonly made in what we would consider an appetizer size, just large enough for one or two bites, but you can make them in a larger turnover-type version. ✳ Samosas are often fried but can also be baked, as they are in this recipe. Traditional samosa dough does not contain yeast and is consequently thinner than most pizza dough, so roll it very thin, as you would a tortilla. A samosa wrapping also generally contains more fat than my Basic Dough, but I find that if I roll the dough out very thin and then brush it lightly with butter, cream, or oil before baking, I get a reasonably authentic result. ✳ Samosas are traditionally made from half-circles of dough folded into cone shapes. If you want to make meal-size samosas, you will use a full dough round to make a turnover, similar to a calzone or piroshki. ✳ Each of the filling recipes should fill 4 large or 16 small samosas generously.

To make appetizer-size samosas, divide the full dough recipe into 8 equal portions and roll them out to make 8 4-inch rounds. (Or, if you are using frozen rounds, thaw and divide each round in half and form each into a ball. Roll the balls out to make 4-inch rounds.)

Cut each of the 8 rounds in half. Dip your finger in water and run it along the cut side of one of the half-rounds. Then make a small cone by overlapping one half of the cut side over the other. Be sure to overlap the sides generously and press them together firmly so the seam won't burst during cooking.

Preheat the toaster oven to 400°F.

1 Basic Dough recipe (page 35), thawed

1 filling recipe from pages 45 and 46

Cream, buttermilk, or olive oil, for brushing

Place 1 or 2 tablespoons of your desired filling into the cone, then carefully and firmly pinch the top closed. Repeat with the rest of the half-rounds. At this point, you can freeze them in a freezer bag for later use.

Using a pastry brush, brush the top of the samosas with cream.

Brush the toaster oven baking tray with oil. Place the samosas on the tray and bake for about 15 minutes, until they are golden brown. Serve warm out of the oven.

To make meal-size samosas, divide the full dough recipe into 2 equal portions. Roll them out to make 2 10-inch rounds. Cut each round in half.

Dip your finger in water and run it along the cut side of one of the half-rounds. Then make a small cone by overlapping one half of the cut side over the other. Be sure to overlap the sides generously and press them together firmly so the seam won't burst during cooking.

Preheat the toaster oven to 400°F.

Place $1/3$ cup of your desired filling into the cone, then carefully and firmly pinch the top closed. Repeat with the rest of the half-rounds. At this point, you can freeze them in a freezer bag for later use.

Using a pastry brush, brush the top of the samosas with cream.

Brush the toaster oven baking tray with oil. Place the samosa on the tray and bake for 20 to 25 minutes, until they are golden brown. Serve warm out of the oven.

To make the keema curry filling, in a large sauté pan over medium-high heat, brown the ground meat and onion, about 10 minutes. Add the garlic, spices, and peas and continue cooking for 3 to 5 minutes more. Season to taste with salt. Proceed with either the appetizer- or meal-size samosa recipe above.

continued

Keema Curry Filling

1 pound lean ground beef or lamb

1 onion, chopped

1 clove garlic, finely minced

$1/4$ teaspoon ground turmeric

$1/4$ teaspoon ground ginger

$1/4$ teaspoon ground cumin

$1/4$ teaspoon ground coriander

$1/4$ teaspoon ground cinnamon

$1/8$ teaspoon chili powder

$1/4$ cup peas, fresh or frozen

Salt

To make the vegetable filling, in a sauté pan over medium heat, melt the butter. Add the onion and cook until browned, about 10 minutes. Add the coriander, cumin, red pepper flakes, and chile and cook for about 3 minutes more. Add the potatoes and peas. Remove from the heat and season to taste with salt. Proceed with either the appetizer- or meal-size samosa recipe above.

Vegetable Filling

2 tablespoons butter or oil

1 onion, chopped

1 teaspoon coriander seeds

1 teaspoon cumin seeds

$1/2$ teaspoon crushed red pepper flakes

1 fresh serrano chile, finely minced

2 large potatoes, boiled, peeled, and finely diced

$1/2$ cup green peas, fresh or frozen

Salt

Beth's Cracked Wheat Bread

MAKES 1 LOAF

My friend Beth Hensperger is a talented bread baker and author of numerous books on baking bread. Although she has created many recipes that I have used and enjoyed, one of my favorites comes from The Bread Bible. This recipe makes a perfect sandwich bread, which is why it is in the lunch chapter, but it also makes great toast for breakfast. ✳ It's important to make sure your toaster oven has a good 2 to 3 inches of room above the loaf pan to allow for the bread to rise. This recipe includes gluten, which helps the bread to rise and makes it fluffy. You can purchase it at health food stores or order it online from www.kingarthurflour.com.

Place the cracked wheat in a large bowl. Pour the boiling water over the cracked wheat. Add the molasses, honey, and butter. With a wooden spoon, gently stir once or twice. Let stand for 1 hour to soften the wheat.

Pour the ingredients through a strainer over a small bowl or measuring cup. Reserve both the liquid and the cracked wheat.

Place the flours and cracked wheat in the bowl of a food processor. With the machine running, gradually add the reserved liquid, buttermilk powder, wheat gluten, salt, and yeast. Continue running the machine until the dough forms a ball.

Generously brush the inside of a large bowl with oil and place the dough in the bowl. Cover the bowl with a damp tea towel and allow the dough to rise in a warm place until it has doubled in size, about 1^1/$_2$ hours.

Brush a standard loaf pan with oil.

continued

^{1}/$_2$ cup cracked wheat

1^1/$_4$ cups boiling water

2 tablespoons molasses

2 teaspoons honey

3 tablespoons unsalted butter

1^1/$_2$ cups unbleached bread flour

1 cup whole wheat flour

^{1}/$_3$ cup dry buttermilk powder

2 tablespoons vital wheat gluten

1^1/$_4$ teaspoons salt

1 package (2^1/$_4$ teaspoons) yeast

After the dough has risen, punch it down. To shape it into a loaf, on a floured work surface, roll the dough out into a rectangle. Then roll up the dough from one long end to the other. Pinch the seam closed, then tuck the ends under gently.

Place the dough in the prepared pan, cover it with a damp tea towel or piece of plastic wrap sprayed with cooking oil, and allow the dough to rise again in a warm place for 30 to 45 minutes, until it has almost doubled in size.

About 5 minutes before the dough has finished rising, preheat the toaster oven to 325°F.

Bake the loaf for about 35 to 40 minutes, until it is golden brown.

Remove the loaf from the toaster oven and allow it to cool for 1 hour before removing it from the pan.

Slice the bread for sandwiches or toast for breakfast. The best way to preserve the flavor and texture of fresh bread is to freeze what you don't eat at the first sitting. To freeze bread, slice it and place the slices in a large freezer bag and pull it out one slice at a time as needed.

Cajun Meatloaf

SERVES 2 TO 4

My neighbor Shirley Tassoni was an internist, a mother, and a very good cook. Her spicy meatloaf, inspired by her culinary hero, Paul Prudhomme, was a neighborhood favorite. Serve this meatloaf with a nice green salad, and then slice the rest for sandwiches on Beth's Cracked Wheat Bread (page 47).

Preheat the toaster oven to 350°F.

Pulverize the red pepper flakes, peppercorns, cumin seeds, salt, and nutmeg in a mortar and pestle, or grind them in an electric coffee mill.

In a large bowl, combine the turkey, ground spices, egg, onion, celery, bell pepper, garlic, Worcestershire sauce, catsup, and bread crumbs. With your hands, mix all of the ingredients thoroughly.

Form the turkey mixture into a loaf.

Brush a loaf pan with oil and place the turkey loaf in it. (You can line the loaf pan with aluminum foil for easy removal. Check your manufacturer's instructions, however, for any cautions against the use of aluminum foil in your toaster oven.)

Bake for 45 minutes, until the top is golden brown and crusty.

Remove the meatloaf from the toaster oven, slice it, and serve hot.

$1/2$ teaspoon red pepper flakes

$1/2$ teaspoon black peppercorns

$1/2$ teaspoon cumin seeds

$1/2$ teaspoon salt

$1/2$ teaspoon ground nutmeg

1 pound lean ground turkey meat

1 egg, lightly beaten

1 onion, finely chopped

2 stalks celery, finely chopped

1 green bell pepper, finely chopped

3 cloves garlic, pressed

1 tablespoon Worcestershire sauce

$1/4$ cup catsup or barbecue sauce

$1/2$ cup bread crumbs

Herbed Oven-Fried Chicken

SERVES 2

You can use boneless, skinless chicken breasts, chicken tenders, or drummettes for this dish. Marinating the chicken in buttermilk overnight makes the chicken extra juicy. Eat it hot right out of the oven, or add it cold to a picnic basket or boxed lunch.

In a shallow dish, mix together the buttermilk, garlic, ¹/₂ teaspoon of the salt, and the oil. Place the chicken pieces in the buttermilk mixture and coat them thoroughly. Marinate the chicken in the buttermilk mixture overnight in the refrigerator.

Preheat the toaster oven to 425°F.

In a food processor, mix the oats, red pepper flakes, the remaining 1 teaspoon salt, Parmesan, and basil. Pulse until the oats are partially powdered. Alternatively, mix the ingredients together in a bowl with a wooden spoon. Place the oat mixture on a plate. Shake any excess buttermilk off the chicken and dredge to coat each piece thoroughly.

For easy clean-up, cover the toaster oven baking tray with aluminum foil and lightly spray it with oil. (Check your manufacturer's instructions, however, for any cautions against the use of aluminum foil in your toaster oven.) Place the chicken pieces on the tray so that they are not touching one another.

Spray the chicken pieces lightly with oil and bake for about 10 to 15 minutes, depending upon the thickness of the meat, until the crust is golden brown and crispy.

Remove the chicken from the toaster oven and serve hot or refrigerate and serve cold over a salad.

¹/₂ cup buttermilk

2 cloves garlic, finely minced

1¹/₂ teaspoons salt

1 tablespoon oil

¹/₂ pound boneless, skinless chicken breasts or chicken tenders

1 cup rolled oats

¹/₂ teaspoon red pepper flakes

¹/₂ cup grated Parmesan cheese

¹/₄ cup fresh basil leaves or rosemary needles

Olive oil spray

Focaccia Doppia

SERVES 1 TO 2

Focaccia doppia is the Italian name for a double-crusted pizza—lots of bread with a yummy filling. Just like a calzone, a focaccia doppia *can be filled with any of the toppings you might use on a pizza; you just use more. Ingredients such as ricotta cheese, ground meat, sausage, fresh or dried mushrooms, onion, fresh spinach, prosciutto, fresh herbs, and Parmesan, cheddar, and mozzarella cheeses work well.*

Mix the salt, yeast, and flours in the bowl of a food processor. Then, with the machine running, slowly pour the water and oil through the feed tube. Add the rosemary. Continue running the machine until the dough forms a ball.

Generously brush the inside of a large bowl with oil and place the dough in the bowl. Cover the bowl with a damp tea towel and allow the dough to rise in a warm place until it has doubled in size, about 1^1/$_2$ hours.

If you do not have a food processor, place the flours in a pile on a wooden work surface. Sprinkle the salt and yeast over the top of the pile. With your fingers form a hollow in the middle of the pile and pour the oil into it. Gradually add the water into the hollow, a few tablespoons at a time, mixing it in with your fingers or a fork. Always incorporate the water from the *inside* of the hollow, so that it doesn't leak through and cause water to run all over your counter. The dough will begin to hold its shape, and you will begin to knead the flour rather than mix it. (The amount of water you will need may vary according to the type of flour you are using.) Knead the dough until it is smooth, shiny, and no

2 teaspoons salt

1 package (2 ^{1}/$_4$ teaspoons) yeast

1 cup whole wheat flour

2 cups all-purpose flour

1^1/$_4$ cups warm water

3 tablespoons olive oil

1 tablespoon chopped fresh
  rosemary needles

Fillings of your choosing (see note)

Olive oil, for brushing

longer sticky. Knead in the rosemary. Place the dough in an oiled bowl, cover it with a damp tea towel or plastic wrap, and let it rise for 1 to 2 hours, until it has doubled in bulk.

Punch the dough down, and then divide it into 4 equal pieces. Each focaccia doppia will use 2 of the rounds. (You can freeze 2 rounds for later use if you are just making 1 serving.) Shape each piece into a disc, then roll each disc out into an 8-inch round.

Preheat the toaster oven to 450°F.

Place the round on your toaster oven baking tray. Arrange the fillings of your choice on top of the dough, leaving about $1/2$ inch free around the edge. Dip your finger in water and run it around the edge of the bottom crust.

Place the top crust over the filling and press the edges of the top and bottom crusts together tightly to seal.

Using kitchen scissors, cut a vent in the top crust. Brush the top of the focaccia lightly with olive oil.

Bake for about 15 minutes, until the crust is golden brown.

Remove the focaccia from the toaster oven and allow it to cool for a few minutes, then cut into halves or quarters and serve.

Savory Open-Faced Turkey, Brie, Gouda, and Sun-Dried Tomato Sandwich

SERVES 1

This very simple recipe comes from my good friend Pascal Vignau, who for eighteen years served as an executive chef at Four Seasons properties around the world. Now he owns a small neighborhood bistro in Encinitas, California, called Savory. Everything he makes is packed with flavor, and this easy sandwich is no exception.

To make the sauce, combine the mustard, ranch dressing, and sun-dried tomatoes in a small bowl.

Preheat the toaster oven to broil.

To assemble the sandwich, place the bread on the toaster oven baking tray and lay the slice of Brie on top. Put the tray in the toaster oven and broil just until the cheese melts on the bread, then remove the tray from the oven.

Place the turkey on top of the melted Brie and drizzle with the sauce.

Top with the Gouda and return the tray to the toaster oven to broil just until the Gouda is melted, about 3 minutes.

Transfer to a plate and serve hot.

Sauce

1 teaspoon Dijon mustard

2 tablespoons ranch dressing

1 tablespoon chopped oil-packed sun-dried tomatoes

Sandwich

1 slice Beth's Cracked Wheat Bread (page 47), or other whole-grain bread

1 slice Brie cheese

2 to 3 thin slices smoked turkey

1 slice Gouda or smoked Gouda

APPETIZERS & SIDES

Here are just enough appetizer recipes to take the edge off the appetite. Just enough nibbles for sitting on the deck with a bottle of wine and a few good friends or for a quiet night in front of the TV for two. I've also included some delicious side dish recipes for those nights when you are entertaining larger groups so you can use your toaster oven to supplement the entrée baking in your big oven.

I have also included drink notes for many of the appetizers. Almost every appetizer in this book would be enhanced by a good bottle of sparkling wine (the domestic equivalent of Champagne, which technically comes only from the Champagne region of France). But then, in my opinion, almost any experience is enhanced by a good bottle of sparkling wine. Salty "bites" almost always pair well with sparkling wines, as anyone who's ever consumed a good bottle with a bowl of potato chips knows.

I have a few domestic favorites, but you could just as easily draw upon the wonderful repertoire of imported French Champagne, cava (Spanish sparkling wine), or prosecco (a delicious Italian sparkler). You could serve the Southwestern Scones (page 72), for instance, with a sparkling wine from Gruet Winery, located (who would believe it?) near Albuquerque, New Mexico. Gruet's vineyards, at an elevation of four thousand feet, are some of the highest in North America, and their prices are more than reasonable. Or you could serve the Artisan Whole Wheat–Walnut Loaf (page 60) with a lively apple-scented glass of Roederer Estate Anderson Valley brut from Mendocino County. Or try a prosecco, the Italian equivalent of Champagne, produced in northern Italy, with the Olive Focaccia (page 66).

Several of the recipes can be frozen to keep quick snacks or treats on hand to bake for guests. For instance, I keep a roll of Cheese Cracker dough (page 59) and several rounds of focaccia in the freezer waiting for just the appropriate moment.

Cheese Crackers

SERVES 2 TO 4

These tasty tidbits are great all by themselves or served with roasted nuts and possibly some olives. Store-bought crackers rarely include such interesting ingredients as fresh, high-quality cheese and nuts in their lineup of ingredients, making these a unique treat.

Place all the ingredients in the bowl of a food processor and pulse until thoroughly mixed and the dough has an even, crumbly texture.

Remove the dough from the processor and quickly knead into a large, smooth ball.

Roll the dough into a long roll or log about 3 inches in diameter. Spray a piece of plastic wrap with cooking spray and wrap the log in it. Refrigerate for at least 1 hour.

Preheat the toaster oven to 350°F.

Slice ¼-inch slices off the roll and place them on your toaster oven baking tray. (If your dough is too crumbly, you can break off walnut-size pieces of dough and flatten them into crackers between the palms of your hands.)

Bake the crackers for about 15 minutes, until they are golden brown. Allow to cool slightly on the tray, transfer to a plate, and serve.

(As with cookie dough, you can bake a few of these crackers, then freeze the rest of the slices on baking sheets. When they are frozen solid, place them in a plastic bag in the freezer and pull them out to bake as needed.)

TO DRINK: Pair these with any good sparkling wine. Yum! Or a nice, flavorful beer would be good, too.

- ½ pound very sharp cheddar, smoked cheddar, or blue cheese, grated
- ½ cup unbleached all-purpose flour
- ½ cup whole wheat pastry flour, freshly milled if possible (see page 16)
- ¼ teaspoon cayenne pepper
- ¼ teaspoon salt
- 3 tablespoons walnut, pecan, or vegetable oil
- ⅓ cup finely chopped walnuts or pecans
- ¾ tablespoon water

Artisan Whole Wheat–Walnut Loaf

MAKES 1 LOAF

Who would imagine that you could bake a free-form artisan loaf of bread in a toaster oven? You can. Serve slices of this loaf with thick slices of Vella Dry Jack cheese or slather it with gobs of Savory Cheesecake (page 64) as a spread. ✳ *Be sure your oven is not only large enough to accommodate the bread pan of your choice, but also has an extra inch of head space for the bread to rise.*

In the bowl of a food processor, combine the whole wheat flour, bread flour, yeast, and salt.

With the machine running, add the water through the feed tube and let the machine run until the water is just mixed in. The dough should be runny, almost batter-like.

Knead in the walnuts for a couple of minutes, using a pastry scraper to help you manage the dough and keep it tidy.

Generously brush the inside of a large bowl with oil and place the dough in the bowl. Cover the bowl with a damp tea towel and allow the dough to rise in a warm place until it has doubled in size, about 2 hours.

For easy clean-up, place a piece of aluminum foil over your toaster oven baking tray and spray it with cooking oil. (Check your manufacturer's instructions for any cautions against the use of aluminum foil in your toaster oven.)

Punch the dough down and form it into an oval shape and transfer it to the baking tray.

2 cups whole wheat flour, freshly milled if possible (see page 15)

1 cup unbleached bread flour

1 package (2¼ teaspoons) yeast

1 teaspoon salt

1¼ cups warm water

1 cup walnuts, coarsely chopped

Spray a piece of plastic wrap with cooking oil and gently place it over the dough. Let the dough rise for another 20 to 30 minutes, until about it rises by about half its size.

About 5 minutes before the bread has finished rising, preheat the toaster oven to 425°F.

Remove the plastic wrap from the loaf and, using a serrated knife, very gently make a slash down the middle of the loaf.

Place the loaf in the toaster oven and bake for about 10 minutes. Turn the heat down to 350°F and continue to bake for about 20 to 25 minutes more, until the loaf is browned and sounds hollow when thumped on the bottom.

Allow the loaf to cool in the pan for at least 30 minutes (if you can stand it) before slicing. You can wrap leftovers in plastic wrap and store in the freezer.

Festive Scones

The less you handle this dough, the lighter your scones will be. Do each step with the idea that you only want to mix the ingredients, not knead them. The dried fruits make them even more festive and interesting.

. . . .

Preheat the toaster oven to 375°F.

In the bowl of a food processor, combine the flour, salt, baking soda, and sugar. Pulse to combine.

Add the cold butter. Turn the machine on and let it run until the butter is just blended in and the dough is the consistency of coarse cornmeal.

Turn the machine off and add the buttermilk, currants, strawberries, and lemon peel. Pulse just long enough to blend the ingredients.

Remove the dough from the processor and knead just a few turns to bring the dough together.

On a floured work surface, roll the dough out until it is about 1 inch thick. Cut 10 to 12 small scones using a biscuit or cookie cutter.

Line the toaster oven baking tray with parchment paper and place the scones on the tray. Bake them for 8 to 10 minutes, until they are golden brown.

Remove the scones from the oven and serve hot. If you have any leftover, freeze them in a plastic bag and reheat for later use.

2 cups all-purpose flour

$1/2$ teaspoon salt

1 teaspoon baking soda

$1/3$ cup sugar

$1/2$ cup (1 stick) cold butter or shortening, cut into pieces

$3/4$ cup buttermilk

2 tablespoons currants

$1/2$ cup chopped dried strawberries

1 tablespoon chopped candied lemon peel

Saganaki

SERVES 2

In the United States, saganaki usually refers to the flaming cheese dish that is served tableside at Greek restaurants. Grilled or sautéed in the kitchen, the dish is then brought to the table, doused with brandy, and then flamed as everyone then shouts, "Opa!" ✳ *In Greece, however, saganaki is a common meze, or appetizer, usually served without all the fanfare. It is fried and brought to the table, almost like a grilled cheese sandwich without the bread. I use the Staube cast-iron pan to give the cheese a nice crust—the 7 1/2-inch Staub roasting pan will accommodate about 6 slices of cheese.*

Spread the flour on a plate. Run each slice of cheese under the tap to moisten it, then dredge in the flour to lightly coat.

Preheat the toaster oven to broil. Heat the butter or olive oil in a small cast-iron pan by placing it in the toaster oven as it preheats. When the oven reaches the broiling temperature, carefully pull out the oven rack and add the cheese slices to the pan.

Broil the cheese slices for about 4 to 5 minutes on one side, until golden, then turn them over and broil for another 4 to 5 minutes. The cheese should be golden brown but not melted.

Drain briefly on paper towels, sprinkle with a bit of paprika, then serve with olives on the side. (One usually uses a fork to eat it.)

TO DRINK: A very cold retsina (Ritinitis, an artisan retsina from Greece, is my favorite) or a chilled New Zealand or Lake County sauvignon blanc.

1/4 cup all-purpose flour

1/4 pound Graviera, kasseri, or feta cheese, cut into 1/2-inch-thick slices

1 tablespoon butter or olive oil

Pinch of sweet paprika

Olives, for serving

Savory Cheesecakes

SERVES 4 TO 6 AS AN APPETIZER, 1 OR 2 AS A LUNCH

While sweet cheesecakes make delicious desserts, savory cheesecakes make excellent appetizers, first courses, or even lunches when eaten hot or cold with a small green salad. They are rich, but well worth the calories now and again. Try spreading this cheesecake on slices of the Artisan Whole Wheat–Walnut Loaf (page 60) for a delicious appetizer.

To make the crust, combine the crackers, butter, cheddar cheese, and walnuts in the bowl of a food processor or blender. Process until they form coarse crumbs.

Divide the crumbs evenly among 4 individual-size springform pans and press them down using a spoon or smooth, round meat pounder.

Preheat the toaster oven to 300°F.

To make the filling, cream together the cream cheese, goat cheese, eggs, feta, cheddar cheese, sour cream, garlic, and thyme with a whisk or a handheld electric mixer until the mixture is light and fluffy.

Divide the mixture among the 4 pans, lightly tapping each pan on the countertop to even out the mixture.

Bake the cheesecakes for 10 minutes, until just golden at the edges. Eat hot out of the oven, or refrigerate for at least 5 hours or overnight before serving.

TO DRINK: Choose from the repertoire of easily available domestic sparkling wines: Roederer Estate, Gloria Ferrar, Domaine Chandon, or Gruet.

Crust

4 (3-inch) whole-grain or water crackers

1 tablespoon butter

1/2 cup grated sharp cheddar cheese

1/4 cup walnuts

Filling

2 (8-ounce) packages cream cheese

1 (11-ounce) package goat cheese

3 eggs

2 ounces feta cheese

1/2 cup grated sharp cheddar cheese

1 cup sour cream

6 cloves garlic, pressed

Leaves from 2 to 3 sprigs fresh thyme

Olive Focaccia

MAKES 4 (8-INCH) ROUNDS

Using the Basic Dough recipe (page 35) from the Lunch chapter, you can make a simple olive focaccia to cut up and serve unembellished, or perhaps with a good cheese and some nuts, as an appetizer. It's a little like pizza without the toppings. Come to think of it, you could add some toppings and make a terrific pizza.

Mix the salt, yeast, and flours in the bowl of a food processor.

Turn the machine on and slowly add the water and oil through the feed tube. Continue running the machine until the dough forms a ball in the food processor.

Transfer the dough to a floured work surface and knead in the olives. Season with pepper to taste.

Generously brush the inside of a large bowl with oil and place the dough in the bowl. Cover the bowl with a damp tea towel and allow the dough to rise in a warm place until it has doubled in size, about $1^1/2$ hours.

Punch the dough down and then divide it into 4 equal pieces. Shape each piece into a disk, then roll each disk out into an 8-inch round. Set 1 aside for the focaccia and place the other 3 in a freezer bag with wax paper between each round and freeze for future use.

Preheat the toaster oven to 400°F.

2 teaspoons salt

1 package ($2^1/4$ teaspoons) yeast

1 cup whole wheat flour

2 cups all-purpose flour

$1^1/4$ cups warm water

3 tablespoons olive oil

$1/3$ cup chopped, pitted kalamata olives

Freshly ground black pepper

Extra virgin olive oil, for brushing

1 tablespoon fresh rosemary needles

Coarse salt, for sprinkling

Lightly brush the toaster oven baking tray with oil. Take the reserved round, stretch it into a rectangle, and place it on the baking tray.

Just before placing the dough in the oven, press it with your fingers to dimple the surface.

Brush the surface of the dough lightly with extra virgin olive oil and sprinkle with the rosemary.

Bake the focaccia for about 10 minutes, until it is golden brown.

Remove the focaccia from the oven and sprinkle lightly with coarse salt. Cut into 6 or 8 squares and serve hot.

TO DRINK: Prosecco, Champagne, or domestic sparkling wine such as Roederer Estate from Mendocino County's Anderson Valley or Gloria Ferrer from Sonoma County's Carneros District.

Braised Scallions

The smell of these simple braised scallions while they are cooking is terrific. Serve them as a side dish wiht Grilled Steak with Cracked Peppercorns (page 98), or serve them cold in a soup or salad.

Preheat the toaster oven to 425°F.

Trim the scallions, cutting away the bottoms and all but 1 inch of the green tops. Combine the olive oil and chicken broth in a shallow bowl and toss the scallions in the mixture to coat. Season the scallions with a grind of salt and pepper.

Place the scallions in an oval or round gratin dish and bake for about 10 minutes, until the tips are slightly blackened.

Top with the crème fraîche and serve hot.

10 scallions

2 teaspoons olive oil

2 tablespoon chicken broth

Freshly ground coarse salt

Freshly ground black pepper

2 tablespoons crème fraîche or
   sour cream

Creamed Spinach

SERVES 2

One of my favorite comfort foods is creamed spinach. As a child, I had it for a special treat on birthdays or trips to San Francisco, where it was served as a side with the world's best fried chicken at Townsend's on Geary.

Heat a wok or frying pan over medium-high heat and add the spinach. Slightly wilt the spinach for 1 minute so you can fit it in the food processor.

Preheat the toaster oven to 350°F.

Transfer the spinach to a food processor or blender and add the crème fraîche. Purée. Add the $1/4$ cup Parmesan cheese, a sprinkle of nutmeg, and salt to taste and pulse a few times to combine.

Mound the spinach mixture in an oval or round 7-inch cast-iron gratin pan and sprinkle with the remaining 2 tablespoons Parmesan cheese.

Bake for about 15 minutes, until the purée is steaming hot. Serve immediately.

1 (12-ounce) bag fresh spinach

$1/2$ cup crème fraîche or sour cream

$1/4$ cup plus 2 tablespoons freshly grated Parmesan cheese

Freshly grated nutmeg

Coarse salt

Roasted Asparagus

SERVES 2

Asparagus can be quickly and easily roasted in the toaster oven while you are preparing the rest of your meal. The cooking time may vary according to the thickness and tenderness of the asparagus stalks. This makes a good accompaniment to almost any grilled meat or fish. Add a dollop of home-made aioli for a special touch.

Preheat the toaster oven to 375°F.

Toss the asparagus with the olive oil and vinegar in an oval baking dish and sprinkle with coarse salt.

Bake for about 20 minutes, until the asparagus spears are tender.

Serve hot as a side dish, or cold in a salad.

10 ounces fresh asparagus, ends trimmed

2 tablespoons olive oil

2 tablespoons balsamic vinegar

Coarse salt

Savory Bread Pudding

SERVES 2

This easy dish can be served as a side for lunch or dinner, or as a meal in itself for breakfast. Allow yourself enough time, as the bread needs to sit for a few hours to become fully saturated with the milk and eggs. This recipe would make an excellent accompaniment to the Grilled Steak with Cracked Peppercorns (page 98), or even served with nothing but a green salad.

Preheat the toaster oven to 350°F. Butter a shallow gratin dish or round roasting pan.

Cut the slices of bread in half diagonally. Arrange them in the prepared pan. Sprinkle the bread slices with the cheese.

In a bowl with a whisk or in a blender, mix the milk, cayenne pepper, and the eggs thoroughly, then pour the mixture over the bread.

Cover and refrigerate for at least 4 hours or overnight to allow the bread to absorb the liquid.

Bake for about 30 minutes, until the bread pudding is golden and puffy. Allow to cool slightly and spoon from the dish to serve.

3 slices whole wheat or sourdough bread

1/2 cup grated cheddar, Gruyère, or smoked Gouda cheese

3/4 cup milk

Pinch of cayenne pepper

3 eggs

Southwestern Scones

SERVES 6

These scones are good for holiday entertaining, as well as for noshing while watching a good movie. The cornmeal, cumin, coriander, and fresh peppers add a Southwestern flair to a classic English treat. They can be enjoyed plain, or serve with garlic or jalapeño jelly.

Preheat the toaster oven to 400°F.

In the bowl of a food processor or in a blender, combine the flour, cornmeal, baking powder, salt, coriander, and cumin. Pulse to blend.

Add the cold butter. Turn on the machine and let run until the butter is just blended in and the dough is the consistency of coarse cornmeal.

Turn the machine off and add the buttermilk and the peppers, then just pulse long enough to blend the ingredients.

Remove the dough from the processor and knead, using just a few turns to bring dough together.

Dust a cutting board with flour and roll the dough out until it is about $1/2$ inch thick. Cut the scones out with a small biscuit or cookie cutter.

Line a toaster oven baking tray with parchment paper. Place the scones on the tray and bake for about 6 to 8 minutes, until they are golden brown.

Remove the scones from oven and serve warm.

Freeze any scones you don't eat and reheat them in your toaster oven for a quick treat. These can also be frozen before baking, then you can pull them out of the bag and throw them in the oven for scones fresh out of the oven.

$1^2/_3$ cups all-purpose flour

$1/_3$ cup cornmeal

1 tablespoon baking powder

1 teaspoon salt

$1/_2$ teaspoon ground coriander

$1/_2$ teaspoon ground cumin

$1/_2$ cup (1 stick) cold butter, cut into pieces

$3/_4$ cup buttermilk

1 tablespoon coarsely chopped red bell pepper

1 tablespoon coarsely chopped jalapeño pepper

Scalloped Potatoes

SERVES 2

Not much is more comforting than a simple side of scalloped potatoes. Whether you prepare them the rich French way with cream or crème fraîche or you use broth instead, they are delicious. I've chosen to make the potatoes with broth instead of the traditional cream because, in my estimation, the dish tastes just as good at half the calories.

Preheat the toaster oven to 375°F. Butter your favorite baking dish (I use a $7^{1}/_{2}$-inch earthenware au gratin pan or a 7-inch round cast-iron roasting pan) with 1 tablespoon of the butter.

Arrange half of the potatoes in one layer on the bottom of the dish. Sprinkle $^{1}/_{2}$ cup of the grated cheese over the potatoes and then arrange the rest of the potato slices on top. Add enough broth to just cover the potatoes. Dot with the remaining tablespoon of butter.

Bake for about 45 minutes, until the stock has been completely absorbed and the potatoes are tender when tested with a knife.

Sprinkle the remaining $^{1}/_{2}$ cup cheese over the potatoes and continue baking until the cheese has turned golden, about 10 minutes.

Cool for a few minutes before serving.

2 tablespoons butter

2 medium russet potatoes, peeled and sliced in $^{1}/_{8}$-inch slices

1 cup grated Gruyère or smoked cheddar cheese

1 cup bouillon or chicken or vegetable broth

Sweet Potato Casserole

SERVES 2

This sweet potato side is great as an accompaniment to pork, roasted chicken, or a traditional Thanksgiving dinner. Top the dish with miniature marshmallows or not, as you deem fit.

Preheat the toaster oven to 375°F.

Bake the sweet potatoes in their jackets until tender when pierced with a fork, about 45 minutes to 1 hour.

Butter a 7-inch round cast-iron roasting pan or a 7$^{1}/_{2}$-inch ceramic dish.

Allow the potatoes to cool slightly, then peel them. Place the potatoes in a bowl and mash the pulp with a potato masher. (I like to leave some texture, but you may prefer your sweet potatoes to be smooth.)

Fold in the currants, butter, pumpkin pie spice, pineapple, and pecans. Place the mixture in the prepared pan.

Bake the casserole for about 20 minutes, until the top is beginning to brown, then cover with marshmallows if using, and bake until the marshmallows are golden, about 10 minutes more. Serve warm.

2 medium sweet potatoes (about 3 cups mashed pulp)

$^{1}/_{4}$ cup currants

2 tablespoons butter

1 teaspoon pumpkin pie spice

$^{1}/_{2}$ cup drained pineapple cubes, coarsely chopped

$^{1}/_{2}$ cup coarsely chopped pecans

1 cup miniature marshmallows (optional)

DINNER

Toaster oven dinners should be easy and yet more imaginative than the standard hot-peanut-butter-sandwich or melted-cheese-on-English-muffins fare. The toaster oven is the perfect tool for cooking dinner when feeling rushed and you want something quick, or in a small quantity, or during those hot summer days when no one wants to light the conventional oven and roast themselves as well as the dinner.

I've tried to keep the recipes in this chapter simple, relying upon good combinations of high-quality ingredients and attractive baking and serving dishes to elevate the simple to the sublime. And as always, serving a good wine or beer with the simplest of dishes can make an enormous contribution to their success. To me, there are very few dishes on which a good wine is wasted. I can even make a great meal of fine red wine, olives, and good bread (hot out of the toaster oven); *nothing* is too simple!

For example, the Eggplant with Tomato and Cream Sauces (page 85) couldn't be easier, but when you choose a nice, fresh eggplant and either homemade or best-quality store-bought tomato sauce (when in a hurry, I get mine from the local pasta shop), then pair the dish with a good Chianti Classico, you have something really special. The Grilled Steak with Cracked Peppercorns (page 98) served with a stuffed potato, green salad, and a bottle of red wine is a sophisticated dinner that can be prepared in just minutes.

Chicken Pot Pie (page 81) and the Macaroni and Cheese with Tapenade (page 88) are the only dishes that really require much of a time commitment, and that only for making a good sauce. (You need to stand over the stove and stir the sauce until it is thick.)

Hopefully, you'll use the recipes in this chapter as a starting point and will go on to experiment on your own, keeping in mind the cardinal rules for toaster oven success: keep it simple, use high-quality ingredients, choose attractive baking and serving dishes, and drink something good with your meal.

Basic Pie Crust Dough

MAKES DOUGH FOR ONE 8¹/₂-INCH QUICHE OR 8-INCH PIE (SINGLE CRUST ONLY),
OR TOP CRUSTS FOR 4 POT PIES.

Learning to make a good basic pie crust is a useful skill. Pie crusts can be used for so many things: chicken, beef, or tuna pot pies; fruit or custard pies; quiches; and tarts. Even though the ingredients are minimal and the instructions and caveats fairly simple, the only thing that will make you proficient at making pie dough is practice. The most important tricks are to keep your ingredients cold and handle the dough as little as possible. Too much handling will most likely yield a cardboard crust. (Making the dough in a food processor is a good way to get the job done while minimizing handling.) Although butter is healthier, I find my pie crusts are flakier and more tender if I use vegetable shortening. The choice is yours. ✳ *My favorite pans for making pies, quiches, and pot pies are the earthenware creations of Karen Tufty at Tufty Ceramics, the cast-iron pieces of Staub, or the colorful pottery cups from Le Creuset. Choose sizes that work with your particular oven.*

. . . .

Place the flour, butter, and salt in the bowl of a food processor. Run the machine until the flour resembles coarse cornmeal and all the lumps of butter have been worked in.

With the machine running, quickly pour the ice water and sugar, if using, into the processor and let the machine run or mix just until the water has been evenly distributed. Your dough may or may not form a ball.

Alternately, if you are making the crust by hand, in a bowl cut the butter into the flour and salt using a pastry cutter or two table knives. Quickly add the ice water and stir just until the water has been evenly distributed.

1¹/₂ cups flour

¹/₂ cup (1 stick) very cold butter, cut into 8 pieces, or ¹/₂ cup vegetable shortening

¹/₂ teaspoon salt

¹/₄ cup ice water

2 tablespoons sugar (for sweet crusts only)

continued

Flour a work surface. Turn the dough out onto the prepared surface and, working quickly, gather it into a disk.

Roll the dough out into a shape that will fit your quiche or pie pan. (Or, if you are using miniature pie or tart pans, you may wish to divide the dough into a suitable number of pieces before rolling each one out.) If you are planning to use the dough for pot pie top crusts, roll out the dough, then cut it with a 3-inch biscuit cutter.

You could actually roll out the dough and cut a bunch of rounds or line the pie dish, then freeze the rounds and/or tart pan on a cookie sheet. Once they are frozen solid, place them in a plastic bag and keep them in the freezer to be pulled out as needed.

Chicken Pot Pies

SERVES 4

These individual pot pies can be made with chicken, turkey, or tuna (canned or fresh), or they can be made with chunky vegetables such as potatoes, parsnips, carrots, celery, and peas for a vegetarian version. A small round of dough sits on top of the filling like a little beret. Fewer carbs, fewer calories than a full crust, but still delicious. You will need four 10-ounce earthenware custard cups. You could also make the entire recipe in one baking dish, if you prefer, and serve up portions at the table.

···

Preheat the toaster oven to 375°F.

To prepare the pot pie filling, melt the butter in a saucepan over medium heat. Add the flour and cook, stirring, for 3 to 5 minutes to brown the flour and butter.

Slowly add the stock to the mixture, whisking constantly. Increase the heat to medium-high and cook the sauce, stirring constantly, until it is thick enough to coat the back of a spoon. Add the carrots, celery, and peas and continue cooking 10 more minutes, until the vegetables are slightly softened. Stir in the parsley, tarragon, and diced chicken. Add a grind or two of fresh nutmeg and season to taste with salt and pepper. Divide the mixture among the custard cups.

To make the top crusts, cut four round caps using a 3-inch biscuit cutter or four 4-inch squares with a knife and place the caps on top of the filling.

Brush the dough with buttermilk or egg white, then bake the pot pies for 15 to 20 minutes, until the top crusts

continued

Pot Pie Filling

2 tablespoons butter

3 tablespoons all-purpose flour

2 cups chicken stock or milk

2 carrots, peeled and sliced (about $2/3$ cup)

1 stalk celery, sliced (about $1/2$ cup)

$1/2$ cup peas, fresh or frozen

1 tablespoon chopped fresh parsley

1 tablespoon coarsely chopped fresh tarragon leaves

2 cups cooked chicken, turkey, or tuna, cut into 1-inch cubes

Freshly ground nutmeg

Salt and freshly ground black pepper

are golden brown. Remove from the oven and allow to cool slightly before serving in the custard cups.

If you have frozen them ahead of time, transfer the pot pies straight from the freezer to the toaster oven and add 10 to 15 minutes to the baking time.

TO DRINK: The light touch of a good dry or off-dry rosé, such as the one from Hart Winery in Temecula, or SoloRosa from winemaker Jeff Morgan, would be a smart choice to complement the creamy sauce and rich crust of the pies. Or perhaps an unoaked chardonnay. These crisp, acidic wines cut through the richness of the crust and the sauce.

Top Crusts

1 recipe Basic Pie Crust Dough (page 79)

Buttermilk or egg white, for brushing

Quiche Lorraine

SERVES 2

My favorite quiche is that made at Bistro Jeanty in Yountville, in the Napa Valley, but chef-owner Philippe Jeanty was working on a cookbook of his own and would not part with his recipe! This is as close as I could come, and I think it's pretty good. This recipe fits Alfred Bakeware's 8½-inch quiche dish perfectly (see Resources, page 118).

Preheat the toaster oven to 400°F.

Roll out the pie crust to fit an 8½-inch quiche dish or pie pan. Place the crust in the dish and crimp the edges using your fingers. Prick the bottom and sides in several places to prevent the crust from bubbling as it bakes.

Place the crust in the toaster oven and bake it for about 15 minutes, until it is lightly golden. Remove the crust from the oven and turn the oven temperature down to 350°F.

In a blender, combine the eggs, sour cream, salt, and nutmeg. Blend until frothy.

Spread the chopped bacon and the grated cheese evenly over the bottom of the pie crust, then gently pour the egg mixture over the top, being careful not to dislodge the bacon or cheese.

Return the quiche to the oven and bake for about 30 to 35 minutes, until the custard is set.

Allow to cool for about 10 to 15 minutes. Using a pastry server, serve slices.

TO DRINK: This would be the time for a traditional Alsatian Pinot Blanc or Gewürztraminer.

1 recipe Basic Pie Crust Dough (page 79)

3 eggs

½ cup sour cream

½ teaspoon salt

Dash of freshly ground nutmeg

3 strips bacon, cooked, well-drained, and chopped

½ cup grated Gruyère or aged Graviera cheese

Eggplant with Tomato and Cream Sauces

SERVES 2

Eggplant, tomatoes, and cheese are a beloved combination of ingredients found in many Mediterranean cuisines during the warmest season of the year. This dish is one very quick, easy way of putting them together.

Preheat the toaster oven to 350°F.

Brush a glass or ceramic baking dish with olive oil. Arrange the eggplant slices in a circular pattern in the dish.

Top the eggplant with the Bolognese sauce, spreading it evenly over the top. Bake for about 30 minutes, until the sauce is bubbly and eggplant slices are tender.

While the eggplant and sauce are baking, whisk the sour cream, garlic, egg, and cheese together thoroughly with a fork in a bowl.

Carefully remove the dish from the oven and add the sour cream mixture.

Return the eggplant to the oven and bake for 15 minutes more, or until the top is lightly browned.

Serve immediately.

TO DRINK: A simple Italian red wine such as a Chianti Classico or Sangiovese.

1 small eggplant, peeled and thinly sliced crosswise into $1/2$-inch pieces

1 cup bottled Bolognese or marinara sauce

$1/2$ cup sour cream

1 clove garlic, minced

1 egg

$1/2$ cup grated Graviera, Parmesan, or mozzarella cheese

Rosemary Lemon Chicken Stuffed with Tapenade

SERVES 2

This dish is a classic throughout the Italian and Greek countryside. Generally, I have the butcher cut a whole chicken into quarters, then I cook two quarters for one meal and freeze the other two for later use. If the capacity of your oven is large enough, you may want to add two potatoes cut into quarters, rubbed with olive oil, and seasoned with salt to the pan. Otherwise, you can serve the chicken with rice or roasted potatoes

To make the tapenade, crush the olives and garlic in a food processor or with a mortar and pestle. Add the olive oil and mix to form a paste.

To prepare the chicken, trim the excess fat from the chicken without removing the skin. Rinse, pat dry, and place the chicken pieces in a ceramic baking dish.

Preheat the toaster oven to 375°F.

Place 2 tablespoons of tapenade under the skin of the breast and stuff some down under the skin of the leg and thigh. Squeeze the juice of the lemon over the chicken. Sprinkle with the rosemary needles and season with salt and pepper.

Bake the chicken, uncovered, for about 45 minutes, until the juices run clear when chicken is pierced with a fork. Remove the chicken from the oven, transfer to a plate, and serve at once.

TO DRINK: The acidity in the lemon may conflict with some wines, so choose a wine with plenty of crisp acidity, such as the artisan retsina from Greece called Ritinitis.

Tapenade

1/2 cup green or black olives, pitted

1 small clove garlic

2 teaspoons olive oil

Rosemary Lemon Chicken

2 chicken quarters, with skin

Juice of 1 lemon

2 tablespoons fresh rosemary needles

Coarse salt and freshly ground black pepper

Yogurt Baked Chicken

SERVES 2

Indian food is one of my favorite cuisines. I love the imaginative combinations of colors, textures, and flavors. This spicy, crusty chicken was inspired by Neela Paniz (the owner of the Bombay Café in Los Angeles, and my favorite Indian restaurant in the world). The chicken will need to marinate for at least four hours or overnight. Serve with fragrant basmati rice and a green salad.

Pound the cinnamon, fennel, cumin, coriander, peppercorns, garlic, and salt in a mortar and pestle until they are quite fine, or grind them in a coffee grinder.

In a bowl, combine the ground spices, chiles, ginger, and yogurt. Stir in the oil.

Place the chicken halves in a baking dish. Spread the yogurt marinade evenly over the top and cover. Allow the chicken to marinate for 4 hours or overnight in the refrigerator.

When you are ready to bake the chicken, preheat the toaster oven to 375°F.

Discard the marinade. Bake the chicken halves uncovered for about 45 minutes, until the juices run clear when the chicken is pierced with a fork.

Remove from the oven, transfer to a plate, and serve at once.

TO DRINK: A chilled dry rosé wine would be a good choice, as would a crisp, acidic white wine, like a chilled viognier, whose light spice and aromatic nose is often a very good choice with the spicy flavors of South Asian foods.

1 small cinnamon stick

1/8 teaspoon fennel seed

1 teaspoon whole cumin seed

1 teaspoon whole coriander seed

4 black peppercorns

6 cloves garlic, pressed

1 teaspoon salt

3 fresh serrano chiles, finely chopped

1 (4-inch) piece ginger, peeled and grated

1 cup plain yogurt

1 tablespoon vegetable oil

1 whole chicken, cut in half and trimmed of all fat

1/4 cup coarsely chopped fresh cilantro

Macaroni and Cheese with Tapenade

SERVES 2

While cheddar cheese is the obvious choice for a dish of traditional mac 'n' cheese, I often jazz it up by using a bit of Greek kasseri, a dash of freshly grated Parmigiano-Reggiano, some smoked Gouda, or Gruyère. As long as the grand total equals 3 cups of flavorful cheese, I'm in business. ✳ *Other favorite additions of mine are halved green olives; diced Canadian bacon or ham; cooked, well-drained, crumbled bacon; sun-dried tomatoes; or tuna and fresh peas. Note that the butter used in a traditional béchamel sauce is missing. This method of making the sauce was taught to me by a teenager who was watching calories. If you follow the instructions and blend the milk and flour in a blender first, you will be amazed at the results. It is just as smooth and thick as a conventional béchamel sauce with half of the calories.* ✳ *Using elegant bakeware can help elevate this dish to a gourmet meal. I use an Alfred Bakeware or Le Creuset stoneware dish.*

To prepare the macaroni and cheese, place the milk and flour in a blender and blend until smooth.

Pour the mixture into a saucepan and cook it over medium-high heat, stirring gently, until the mixture is thick enough to coat the back of a spoon, about 10 to 15 minutes.

When the sauce has thickened, add the cheese, one cup at a time, stirring gently after each addition, until melted. Remove from the heat.

Preheat the toaster oven to 350°F.

Butter a 7- or 8-inch gratin dish.

In a large bowl, gently mix the cheese sauce (and any other ingredients you may wish to add) with the macaroni.

continued

Macaroni and Cheese

3 cups milk

6 tablespoons all-purpose flour

3 cups grated cheese

4 cups macaroni or penne, cooked al dente

Transfer the macaroni and cheese to the prepared dish and bake uncovered for 15 or 20 minutes, until the top is golden brown.

To make the tapenade, while the macaroni and cheese is baking, prepare the tapenade. Mash the olives, garlic, oil, pepper, and lemon juice with a mortar and pestle, or give them a whir in a mini-processor, leaving some texture to keep things lively.

Remove the macaroni and cheese from the oven and spoon a generous dab of tapenade on the top. Serve warm.

TO DRINK: Choosing an appropriate beverage for macaroni and cheese will depend upon the type of cheese you choose to use in the recipe. A classic sharp cheddar might best be paired with a nice gutsy beer. But other cheeses, such as a blue cheese of some type, might call for a Bordeaux red or a Central Coast Syrah.

Tapenade

$1/2$ cup black or green olives, pitted

1 clove garlic, pressed

2 tablespoons olive oil

Freshly ground black pepper

Dash of freshly squeezed lemon juice

Broiled Peanut Chicken Skewers

SERVES 2

These broiled chicken skewers are delicious simply served with rice and a salad. Or, for a delicious alternative, you can slide the broiled chicken pieces off the skewer onto a whole wheat tortilla or chapati, top them with some thick, creamy yogurt and shredded lettuce or spinach, and eat out of hand like a soft taco. Plan ahead to marinate the chicken overnight or for at least a few hours before cooking.

In a bowl or a food processor, thoroughly combine the peanut butter, peanut oil, vinegar, tamari, lemon juice, garlic, and ginger.

Cut the chicken into bite-size pieces (about 1^1/$_2$-inch cubes) and mix the chicken pieces in a bowl with the peanut sauce. Marinate the chicken for at least 4 hours or overnight. Meanwhile, soak 4 wooden skewers in water to prevent them from burning later in the toaster oven.

After the chicken has marinated, preheat the toaster oven to broil. Thread the marinated chicken pieces on the wooden skewers. Discard the marinade.

Broil the chicken skewers on one side for about 8 minutes, until browned, then turn them over and broil them on the other side for about 5 minutes, until the edges of the chicken are blackened.

Remove from the oven, transfer the skewers to a plate, and serve hot.

TO DRINK: This is one of those dishes that cries out "fire and ice." I'd serve a very well chilled glass of Sauvignon Blanc, or perhaps Pinot Blanc or even Viognier. Just make sure it is good and cold.

^{1}/$_2$ cup chunky peanut butter

^{1}/$_2$ cup peanut oil

^{1}/$_4$ cup apple cider vinegar

^{1}/$_4$ cup tamari

^{1}/$_4$ cup freshly squeezed lemon juice

4 to 6 cloves garlic, pressed

1 (1-inch) piece of fresh ginger, peeled and grated

2 boneless and skinless chicken breasts

^{1}/$_4$ cup coarsely chopped fresh cilantro

Grilled Salmon with Basil-Garlic Butter

SERVES 2

The very best salmon I've ever tasted was plucked from the Monterey Bay the morning I ate it, cooked over an open campfire in Big Sur, and served with only a dab of basil-flavored butter. This is a similar recipe minus the campfire. It works as well with fresh halibut, tuna, or bass as it does with salmon; the only requirement is that the fish be impeccably fresh. ✳ *This recipe makes more basil butter than is needed, but it is easier to make a whole stick of herb butter and freeze some of it for later use. It can be used on pasta or grilled meats, or spread on freshly baked bread. The basil butter needs to be refrigerated for at least a few hours or overnight to harden and let the flavors meld. I have also provided a variation for olive butter below.*

....

To make the basil-garlic butter, blend the butter, basil, and garlic together in a bowl with a fork until thoroughly mixed. Refrigerate for several hours or overnight before using.

About 5 minutes before you are ready to prepare the fish, preheat the toaster oven to broil. For easy clean up, line the toaster oven baking tray with aluminum foil. (Check your manufacturer's instructions, however, for any cautions against the use of aluminum foil in your toaster oven.)

To prepare the salmon, lay the fish on the prepared tray. Place the salmon under the broiler and cook for about 8 minutes on each side, until the fish turns opaque orange. (The cooking time may vary depending upon the thickness of your fish.)

Basil-Garlic Butter

1/2 cup (1 stick) butter, at room temperature

2 tablespoons chopped fresh basil

2 cloves garlic, pressed

Salmon

2 (4-ounce) fillets fresh salmon

Coarse salt

1 fresh lemon wedge

continued

Remove the salmon from the toaster oven, transfer to a plate, and top it with a generous dab of the basil-garlic butter. The leftover basil butter can be stored in the refrigerator or freezer.

To make the olive butter, blend the butter, mustard, olives, and garlic together in a bowl with a fork until thoroughly mixed. Refrigerate for several hours or overnight before using.

Any extra butter can be stored in the refrigerator for later use on pasta or grilled fish or meats.

TO DRINK: Pinot Noir is almost always a good choice with salmon. In fact, each year at the Oregon International Pinot Noir Celebration's final night feast, an estimated 600 pounds of salmon is served, washed down with many bottles of delicious Oregon Pinot Noir.

Olive Butter

$^1/_2$ cup (1 stick) unsalted butter, at room temperature

2 teaspoons Dijon mustard

2 tablespoons pitted and chopped kalamata olives

2 cloves garlic, pressed

Scallops with Pancetta and Saffron

SERVES 2

This simple and satisfying dish might well be found in a Spanish tapas bar. To me, eating tapas in Spain or mezes in Greece is a very civilized custom. Conversation, punctuated by small bites of interesting food and good local wine, takes the place of the more common American focus on simply "getting the job done" at the table. ✳ You can also use this recipe and technique with large shrimp instead of scallops or with a combination of the two with equally delicious results. ✳ And for you gardeners, saffron crocus are fairly easy to grow. I have many all over my garden that poke their beautiful royal purple heads up when the rain comes and the weather warms up in the fall. To harvest them, you pull out the saffron-colored stamen by hand and lay them on a paper towel to dry before storing them in a small glass jar.

Preheat the toaster oven to 400°F. Heat the oil in a small, round cast-iron pan by placing it in the toaster oven as it preheats. (For tapas, you can also serve the dish in the pan.)

When the toaster oven is fully heated, carefully pull the pan out of the oven with heavy oven mitts and add the parsley, saffron, scallops, and pancetta and mix together.

Return the pan to the oven and bake for 5 to 7 minutes, until the scallops are cooked. Remove the pan from the oven, add the sherry to the pan, and toss the scallops to coat.

Transfer to a plate or serve immediately in the cast-iron pan.

2 tablespoons olive oil

2 tablespoons finely chopped fresh parsley

Several strands saffron

1/2 pound scallops

2 tablespoons diced pancetta

1 tablespoon dry sherry or white wine

Turkey, Tarragon, and Apple Meatloaf

SERVES 2

Meatloaf is a quintessential American comfort food. This lean loaf combines the holiday flavors of turkey, apples, and allspice, and is topped with a beautifully shiny apple jelly glaze. I like to make two mounded individual meatloaves from this recipe, then unmold them and serve them on plates with a mountain of mashed or scalloped potatoes.

· ·

Preheat the toaster oven to 350°F.

To make the meatloaf, crush the allspice berries and peppercorns in a mortar with a pestle, or grind them in a coffee mill.

Place the turkey, bread crumbs, onion, apple, parsley, egg, tarragon, salt, catsup, mustard, and the crushed pepper and allspice berries in a large bowl. Thoroughly combine all the ingredients with your hands.

Spray the bottom and sides of two 10-ounce custard cups, (or four 4- to 5-ounce cups, or one loaf pan) with oil.

Divide the turkey mixture in half (or in as many portions as needed to fit your pans) and form each half into a ball. Place the balls into the prepared cups, so that the tops are mounded. Place the cups on the toaster oven baking tray.

Meatloaf

6 allspice berries

4 peppercorns

1 pound lean ground turkey

$1/2$ cup fresh bread crumbs

$1/2$ large onion, finely chopped

$1/2$ Granny Smith apple, unpeeled, cored, and chopped

$1/4$ cup chopped fresh parsley

1 egg, lightly beaten

2 tablespoons chopped fresh tarragon

1 teaspoon salt

$1/4$ cup catsup

2 teaspoons prepared mustard

To make the apple jelly glaze, mix the jelly, catsup, allspice, and cayenne pepper together in a bowl. Using a pastry brush, paint the glaze mixture over each meatloaf. (You may also wish to pull the oven rack out carefully and brush the loaves once or twice while they are baking.)

Bake the loaves for about 25 minutes, until nicely browned on top. (The baking time will vary if you use smaller cups or form one loaf.) Serve hot out of the oven.

TO DRINK: Gewürztraminer is a German grape variety with which few Americans are familiar. Its name means "spicy traminer," because it has subtle spicy aromas and flavors. British Columbia's Okanagan Valley produces some stunning crisp, aromatic Gewürztraminers. If you can find one, try it. Better yet, go visit the region and bring some home with you. If that doesn't work, opt for a domestic "Gewürzt," as it is sometimes called for short. The spiciness of the wine might complement the apple and spices in the meatloaf.

Apple Jelly Glaze

$1/4$ cup apple, cherry, pomegranate, or red currant jelly

2 tablespoons catsup, chili, or barbecue sauce

Pinch of ground allspice

Pinch of ground cayenne pepper

Grilled Steak with Cracked Peppercorns

SERVES 2

During the time I was writing this book, our beloved Julia Child passed away. The world had been made a happier place because of her. She drew our attention to the great care traditionally taken by the French in food preparation. Shortly after she died, I found an old copy of Julia Child's Kitchen *and I spent a lazy afternoon thumbing through its pages, perusing those simple classic French dishes and enjoying Julia's kitchen wisdom.* ✳ *Though I rarely eat steak these days, I enjoy a good one as a special treat now and again, and I felt newly inspired by Julia's simple instructions for sautéing a steak in the pan.* ✳ *"Why not try it in the broiler of my toaster oven?" I thought. "Why not?" I could hear her say. Followed by "Num, num, num!"*

Preheat the toaster oven to broil (the oven should be good and hot before you put the steak in the oven). For easy clean-up, line the toaster oven baking tray with aluminum foil. (Check your manufacturer's instructions, however, for any cautions against the use of aluminum foil in your toaster oven.)

Crush the peppercorns and salt in a mortar using a pestle. Rub both sides of the steak with the olive oil and press the peppercorn mixture into the steaks.

Place the steak on the prepared tray. Place the steak under the broiler and cook for about 7 to 10 minutes on each side, until the steak reaches medium doneness. (The time may vary depending upon the thickness of the steak you have chosen and the degree of doneness you prefer.) Remove from the oven, transfer to plates, and serve immediately with lemon.

TO DRINK: I love the lusty, chewy wines of Michel-Schlumberger Winery in Dry Creek Valley. Either their cabernet sauvignon or merlot would go beautifully with this.

- 4 teaspoons black or mixed peppercorns
- 1 to 2 teaspoons coarse salt
- 2 Porterhouse steaks (or other cut of choice)
- 2 tablespoons extra-virgin olive oil
- 2 lemon wedges (optional)

TEA & GOODIES

When it comes to toaster oven desserts, you've got some interesting options, including mini- or individual-sized desserts in a variety of pans and dishes. From cookies to apple crisp, with a toaster oven you can have an endless supply of desserts hot out of the oven.

One of my favorite tricks is to use small cake pans. For example, I make the carrot cake in individual-size Bundt cake pans and I use personal-size springform cake pans for making small cheesecakes and glass or earthenware custard cups for custards and puddings. If your toaster oven is large enough, you might be able to fit one of the 6-portion decorative cake tins that are sold at many specialty stores.

If there are only two of you, you can easily eat two chocolate cheesecakes and freeze the other two for a special treat some night when you just don't have it in you to bake!

The toaster oven is perfect for baking cookies one or two at a time, so you can eat fresh cookies hot out of the oven anytime. The cookie recipes in this chapter reflect this easy strategy. I suggest making a batch of cookie dough and then placing the individual cookies on a cookie sheet, as if you were going to bake them, but freezing them instead. When they are frozen solid, you can take the unbaked cookies off the cookie sheet and throw them into a freezer bag and store them in your freezer. (If you throw them into the bag without freezing them first, they will only stick together in one big glop.) Then, whenever you want freshly baked cookies, simply take one or two out of your freezer and bake them in your toaster oven. Of course, you will surely want to bake a few for eating on the spot!

Once you get the hang of baking in your toaster oven, you can easily adapt just about any favorite recipe to the toaster oven and then enjoy your own personal favorites any time you like.

Anzacs

MAKES 12 (3-INCH) COOKIES

ANZAC is an acronym for the Australian–New Zealand Army Corps, a camaraderie of the combined forces of the two countries that made its debut in WWI. These cookies were baked by the women of New Zealand and Australia for their men abroad. They have a wonderful texture and flavor from the coconut and oats, and they keep well.

Combine the flour, coconut, sugar, and oats in a large bowl and mix well. In a small saucepan or in a glass dish in the microwave, melt the butter with the water, baking soda, and syrup. Add the butter mixture to the dry ingredients and mix well with your hands.

Use a soup spoon to scoop the dough and form each scoop into a ball with your hands and place them on an ungreased baking sheet. Freeze the unbaked cookie balls on the sheet. After they are frozen, place them in a plastic freezer bag and store them in your freezer.

Whenever you want freshly baked cookies, simply pull 1 or 2 frozen cookies out of the freezer and bake them in your toaster oven at 350°F for about 20 minutes, until they are golden brown. Allow to cool for a few minutes on the tray before serving.

1 cup all-purpose flour

1 cup unsweetened coconut

1 cup brown sugar

1 cup rolled oats

$1/2$ cup (1 stick) butter

2 tablespoons water

$1/2$ teaspoon baking soda

1 tablespoon golden syrup, molasses, or honey

Carrot Cakes with Lemon Glaze

SERVES 4

This carrot cake is full of fiber and flavor and is lightly sweetened with pineapple, coconut, currants, and nuts. ✳ *Cream cheese frosting is traditional with carrot cake, but for a change, this recipe calls for a lemon glaze.*

Preheat the toaster oven to 325°F.

To make the carrot cake, mix the flour, sugar, baking soda, and cinnamon together in a large mixing bowl. In a separate small bowl, whisk together the egg, oil, and buttermilk.

Blend the liquid ingredients into the dry and stir just until mixed. Add the carrots, pineapple, coconut, nuts, and currants and stir just until mixed in.

Divide the batter among 4 mini Bundt cake pans (or similar individual-size pans).

Bake for 20 minutes, or until a toothpick inserted in the cake comes out clean.

To make the lemon glaze, while the cakes are baking, mix the powdered sugar, lemon juice, and lemon zest together in a small bowl. Cover a cake rack with a tea towel or foil.

When the cakes have finished baking, remove them from the toaster oven and allow them to cool in their pans. When they have cooled, pop them out of the pans and set them on the prepared rack. Drizzle the glaze evenly over the cakes.

Allow the glaze to harden, about 5 minutes, then serve topped with the walnuts.

Carrot Cakes

1 cup all-purpose flour

1/3 cup brown sugar

1 teaspoon baking soda

1 teaspoon ground cinnamon

1 egg

2 tablespoons oil

3/4 cup buttermilk

3/4 cup grated carrots

1/4 cup crushed pineapple, well drained

1/4 cup unsweetened shredded coconut

1/2 cup coarsely chopped nuts

1/4 cup currants

Lemon Glaze

1 cup powdered sugar

3 tablespoons lemon juice

Zest from 1 lemon

2 tablespoons chopped toasted walnuts or almond slices, for garnish

Chocolate Cheesecakes

These little gems are so rich you will want to save them for a very special occasion. Because they cook for such a short time, you can add tiny marshmallows to make "Rocky Road" cheesecakes. If you don't like Lorna Doone cookies, then by all means use Oreos or chocolate wafers of some kind.

Preheat the toaster oven to 325°F.

To make the crust, blend the cookies, walnuts, and butter in a food processor until they form a mixture with a coarse, even texture.

Spray 4 mini nonstick cheesecake pans with oil. Divide the mixture evenly among the prepared pans and press it down into the pans with a spoon or round meat pounder to form the crust.

To make the filling, place the baking chocolate in a baking dish and place it in the preheating oven to melt it.

Using a whisk, mixer, or food processor, beat the cream cheese, sugar, melted chocolate, maple flavoring, espresso, and sour cream until relatively light and fluffy. Beat in the eggs one at a time, and then add the walnuts and chocolate chips and mix thoroughly.

Divide the mixture evenly among the prepared pans. Tap the pans against the counter or a cutting board to evenly distribute the mixture in the pans and to remove any air bubbles.

Crust

12 Lorna Doone cookies, crushed

1 tablespoon butter

$1/4$ cup walnuts

Filling

8 ounces semisweet baking chocolate

$2 1/2$ (8-ounce) packages cream cheese, at room temperature

$1/2$ cup sugar

1 teaspoon maple flavoring

1 tablespoon finely ground espresso

1 cup sour cream

3 eggs

1 cup walnuts

1 cup semisweet chocolate chips

Raspberries, for serving (optional)

Place the pans in the oven and bake for about 10 minutes, until the batter is slightly puffed at the edges. Do not overbake.

Remove the cheesecakes carefully from the oven and allow them to cool on a wire rack for 45 minutes, then chill them in the refrigerator for at least 5 hours before attempting to unmold them. Remove the sides of the pan and use a spatula to transfer the cheesecakes from the bottom of the pan to a plate. Add a few fresh raspberries on the side or top and serve.

TO DRINK: Serve with either an icewine from Canada's Okanagan Valley or a delicious muscat from Samos Coop.

Chocolate Lava Cakes

SERVES 4

I call these treats "lava cakes" because, when properly baked, their insides are still gooey and ooze out when you cut or bite into them. These cakes are an exception to the clean-toothpick rule: be careful not to overcook them, or they will be dry and unappetizing. Grind the walnuts in a coffee mill or food processor.

Preheat the toaster oven to 150°F. Generously butter 4 cups of a 6-cup muffin tin and then dust it with the ground walnuts.

To make the chocolate lava cakes, place the chocolate squares and the ¼ cup butter in an ovenproof dish and melt them in your toaster oven while you prepare the other ingredients.

Combine the flour, baking soda, sugar, and salt in a large bowl. In a smaller bowl, whisk the buttermilk and eggs together, and then stir them into the dry ingredients.

Slowly add the melted chocolate and butter to the batter, blending thoroughly. Add the chocolate chips and walnuts and stir until they are evenly distributed.

Increase the oven temperature to 350°F. Pour the batter evenly into the prepared muffin tin and, once the oven has reached the correct temperature, bake the cakes for 10 minutes.

continued

Chocolate Lava Cakes

¼ cup (½ stick) unsalted butter, plus more for preparing pans

⅛ cup finely ground walnuts

3 (1-ounce) squares unsweetened chocolate

3 (1-ounce) squares semisweet chocolate

½ cup all-purpose flour

½ teaspoon baking soda

½ cup sugar

¼ teaspoon salt

2 tablespoons buttermilk

2 eggs

½ cup semisweet chocolate chips

½ chopped walnuts

To make the raspberry coulis, while the cakes are baking, purée the raspberries and sugar in a blender, until they form a nice, thick sauce.

Remove the cakes from the oven and carefully remove them from the tin. Serve them with a sprinkle of powdered sugar and dollop of softly whipped cream over the top and the raspberry coulis on the side.

✳ Note: Melting chocolate in a toaster oven on low heat (about 150°F) works beautifully. There is no need to watch it constantly or to use the cumbersome bain marie technique.

TO DRINK: You could serve these delicious cakes with Bonny Doon Vineyard's Framboise, a delightful, raspberry dessert wine, or, if you prefer, with a good glass of cold milk.

Raspberry Coulis

1 cup raspberries, fresh or frozen

$1/2$ cup sugar

Powdered sugar, for topping

Whipped cream, for topping (optional)

Old-Fashioned Apple Crisp

SERVES 2

Several years ago I planted a dwarf apple tree in my backyard. Every year, without fail, the tree gives me many small, juicy apples with precisely the right balance of sugar and acid. I eat as many as I can right off the tree, but sometimes there are just too many and then I revert to this classic recipe. ✳ *Baking it in either the Tufty ceramic bakeware or a cast-iron pan gives it a delicious crust.*

Preheat the toaster oven to 325°F.

To make the apple filling, toss the apple slices, cinnamon, and cloves together in a bowl. (If your apples are tart or you prefer sweeter desserts, add up to a few tablespoons of sugar. Conversely, if your apples lack the right amount of tartness, add a dash of lemon juice.)

Spread the apples evenly in your baking dish. (I use a $7^1/_2$-inch round cast-iron baking dish.)

To make the crisp topping, add the flour, brown sugar, cinnamon, cloves, and butter to the bowl of a food processor and process them until the butter is in pea-size pieces. Alternatively, in a bowl, cut them together using two knives or a pastry cutter. Add the oats and walnuts and pulse or mix just until combined.

Spread the crisp mixture evenly over the apples.

Bake for about 20 minutes, until the topping is crispy and brown and the apple slices are tender. (The cooking time may vary with the thickness of your apple slices.)

Spoon onto small plates and serve warm topped with ice cream or whipped cream.

Apple Filling

2 apples, peeled, cored, and thinly sliced

$^1/_2$ teaspoon ground cinnamon

$^1/_4$ teaspoon ground cloves

1 to 2 tablespoons sugar (optional)

Dash of lemon juice (optional)

Crisp Topping

$^1/_4$ cup all-purpose flour

$^1/_4$ cup dark brown sugar

$^1/_2$ teaspoon ground cinnamon

$^1/_4$ teaspoon ground cloves

1 tablespoon unsalted butter

$^1/_4$ cup rolled oats

$^1/_2$ cup walnuts

Ice cream or whipped cream, for topping

Honey Custard

SERVES 4

Plain vanilla custard is one of my favorite comfort foods, especially when it's made with fresh organic milk and eggs and some sort of wild honey. Trying to find milk with any flavor at all is a challenge these days, since most commercial dairy cows are fed a steady diet of grain and are never allowed to graze in a pasture. This is convenient for the farmer, but not much fun for the cows, and it makes for boring, flavorless milk. See if you can find some "real" milk from some "real" cows, and your custard will be the better for it.

Preheat the toaster oven to 325°F.

Blend all of the ingredients together in a blender.

Place four 10-ounce custard cups in a 9-inch baking pan or 2 loaf pans. Pour the custard mixture into the cups.

Using a measuring cup, pour hot tap water into the baking pan until it comes about three-quarters of the way up the sides of the custard cups.

Carefully place the baking dish in the toaster oven and bake for about 25 minutes. Carefully remove the cups from the water bath and allow to cool for an hour at room temperature. Refrigerate for at least 4 hours before serving in the custard cups.

1 quart organic milk

$^1/_2$ cup honey

6 eggs

1 tablespoon vanilla

Lemon Verbena Strawberry Shortcake

SERVES 6

Aside from lemon itself, lemon verbena is perhaps the most "lemony" citizen of the plant kingdom. As with biscuits or scones, shortbread of this type is best made in a food processor, which quickly and efficiently accomplishes the job of cutting in the butter.

Place the sliced strawberries in a bowl and cover with the sugar. Allow to marinate for 2 hours.

After the strawberries have marinated, preheat the toaster oven to 400°F.

In the bowl of a food processor or in a blender, mix the flour, salt, baking powder, baking soda, lemon verbena, and butter until there are no lumps of butter left and the mixture is the texture of coarse meal. Remove the lid and add the buttermilk all at once. Pulse just enough to blend all the ingredients (do not let the machine run).

Lightly flour a work surface. Turn the very dry dough out and gather it together into a flat disk with your hands, handling it as little as possible.

Roll the dough out until it is 1 inch thick. Using a 3-inch biscuit cutter, cut 6 rounds out of the dough.

Place the rounds on your toaster oven baking tray and bake for about 10 minutes, until they are golden.

Remove the biscuits from the oven. Allow them to cool slightly, then slice them in half using a serrated knife.

Arrange the biscuit bottoms on a plates. Pour $1/2$ cup of the strawberries over each, then cover with the biscuit tops, placing each slightly askance over the bottom. Top with a dollop of whipped cream and serve warm.

3 cups sliced fresh strawberries

$1/2$ cup sugar

2 cups unbleached flour

$1/2$ teaspoon salt

2 teaspoons baking powder

$1/2$ teaspoon baking soda

2 tablespoons grated lemon verbena or lemon peel

$1/2$ cup (1 stick) butter, cut into pieces

$2/3$ cup buttermilk

Whipped cream, for topping

Peanut Butter Cookies

MAKES 12 (3-INCH) COOKIES

These peanut butter cookies are subtly sweetened, like European cookies or biscuits. You can sprinkle the tops with a pinch or two of sugar before baking if you prefer a sweeter dough. For an afternoon break, I like to bake two and eat them hot out of the oven with a glass of milk or cup of tea.

Cream the butter, peanut butter, brown sugar, vanilla, and eggs together in a bowl by hand or with a handheld mixer or in a food processor.

In another bowl, mix the flour, salt, baking soda, and peanuts together thoroughly.

Mix the dry ingredients into the peanut butter mixture, then form the dough into golf ball–size pieces. Press the cookies flat on an ungreased cookie sheet using a fork or your fingers.

Freeze the unbaked cookies on the cookie sheets. Once they have hardened, pack them in a plastic freezer bag and store them in the freezer.

Whenever you want freshly baked cookies, simply pull 1 or 2 frozen cookies out of the freezer, sprinkle them with sugar, and bake them in your toaster oven at 350°F for about 12 minutes, or until edges are lightly browned. Remove from the oven and serve.

TO DRINK: A nice, cold glass of milk is the perfect accompaniment.

1 cup (2 sticks) butter

1 cup peanut butter

1 cup brown sugar

1 tablespoon vanilla

2 eggs

2 cups all-purpose flour

$1/4$ teaspoon salt

$1^1/2$ teaspoons baking soda

1 cup chopped dry roasted peanuts, preferably unsalted

Sugar for sprinkling

Personal Cheesecakes

SERVES 4

I can easily fit 4 mini cheesecake pans (available at most cookware shops for under $5) in my toaster oven. This classic cheesecake would be delicious topped with fresh sliced strawberries, raspberries, apricots, or peaches.

Preheat the toaster oven to 300°F.

To make the crust, blend the graham crackers and butter in a food processor until they have a coarse, even texture. Or place the graham crackers between two sheets of wax paper and roll them into crumbs with a rolling pin.

Spray 4 mini nonstick cheesecake pans with oil. Divide the crust mixture evenly among the prepared pans. Press the graham cracker crust mixture down into the pans.

To make the filling, using a whisk, mixer, or food processor, beat the cream cheese, sugar, vanilla, and sour cream until thoroughly mixed. Beat in the eggs one at a time.

When the eggs have been thoroughly blended, divide the mixture evenly among the prepared pans. Gently tap the pans on the counter or a cutting board to evenly distribute the mixture in the pan and remove any air bubbles.

Place the pans in oven and bake the cheesecakes for about 10 minutes, until just set and the edges are slightly puffed. Do not overbake.

Remove the cheesecakes from the oven and allow them to cool on a wire rack for about 45 minutes, then chill them in the refrigerator for at least 5 hours before attempting to unmold them. Place each cheesecake on a plate and serve with a fresh strawberry fanned out over the top.

Crust

4 graham crackers

1 tablespoon butter

Filling

3 (8-ounce) packages cream cheese, at room temperature

1/2 cup sugar

1 tablespoon vanilla

1 cup sour cream

3 eggs

Fresh strawberries, for garnishing

Pecan Cookies

MAKES 12 (3-INCH) COOKIES

My friend Susan Johnson's cooking had become the subject of much merriment among her eight children. "Mommie burns everything," the kids would chime. But this was one of her truly great recipes, enjoyed by all her neighbors and kids alike. These cookies have a beautiful pecan flavor and a light texture.

Preheat the toaster oven to 350°F.

Cream the butter, granulated sugar, and 1 cup of the powdered sugar together using a mixer or food processor. Blend in the vanilla and flour, then add the nuts and mix until blended.

Shape the dough into walnut-sized balls and flatten them with the tips of your fingers on an ungreased cookie sheet. Freeze the cookies on the sheet, and after they are frozen, pack them in a plastic freezer bag and store in your freezer.

Whenever you want freshly baked cookies, simply pull 1 or 2 frozen cookies out of the freezer and bake them in your toaster oven at 350°F for 10 minutes, or until they are golden brown.

Sprinkle the cookies with powdered sugar while still warm.

1 cup (2 sticks) butter

4 tablespoons granulated sugar

1 cup powdered sugar, plus more for sprinkling

2 teaspoons vanilla

2 cups all-purpose flour

1$\frac{1}{2}$ cups pecans, chopped

One of the ways to elevate toaster oven meals from the ordinary to the upscale is simply to choose bakeware that is attractive and functional, something just a little fancier than typical aluminum or glass. The following is a list of companies I have found that make unique cookware in sizes and shapes that work well in a toaster oven.

Staub Cast-Iron Cookware

The Staub family has been making enameled cast-iron cookware in Alsace, France, for thirty years. Staub pieces are beautifully designed and practical. Aside from being finished with a unique matte-enamel finish that makes cleanup easy, Staub cast iron gives a beautiful golden crust to many of my favorite dishes. Many of the smaller dishes can go directly from the toaster oven to the table. I cannot recommend these attractive yet functional pieces of bakeware highly enough. The only caveat is that one must always handle cast iron carefully, being mindful that it gets mightily hot in the oven and can burn you badly if you are not paying attention. I would never let a child handle cast-iron cookware. Check the Staub USA website for more product information, photos, use, and care. My personal favorites are the small oval and round roasting pans.

www.staubusa.com

Alfred Bakeware

Karen Tufty, owner of Tufty Ceramics and maker of Alfred Bakeware, began making ceramic bakeware in 1986 from red clay mined in upstate New York. It is called Alfred Bakeware after the town in which it is mined and made, as well as after Alfred University, in whose ceramics department the bakeware was first made.

The secret to Alfred Bakeware's nonstick seal is not a glaze but rather a "terra sigillata" coating that simulates a process used by American Indians who burnished their unfired pottery by rubbing it with a stone. To produce the finish, crushed Alfred pottery is placed in a water formula to dissolve it, then it is sprayed back on the pottery surface, filling microscopic nooks and crannies and creating the bakeware's ultrasmooth nonstick finish.

I love the look of these beautiful reddish clay pans and make constant use of the au gratin pan, square baking pan, quiche dish, and loaf pans (both mini and standard). Like the cast-iron cookware, the Alfred Bakeware makes a wonderful crust, especially on breads.

For more information about Alfred Bakeware see Tufty's website:

www.tuftyceramics.com

Le Creuset

Although the Le Creuset company is best known for its brightly colored, high-quality enameled cast-iron cookware, it also makes a line of brightly colored stoneware baking dishes, ramekins, custard cups, and individual soup crocks. Plenty of their pieces are small enough to fit in a toaster oven, and because they are available in designer kitchen colors, they can easily go from the toaster oven to the table.

I have made good use of their custard cups, soup crocks, ramekins, and au gratin dishes for desserts, custards, flan, scalloped potatoes, and casseroles.

Check out Le Creuset bakeware, both cast iron and stoneware, at their website:

www.lecreuset.com

Penzeys Spices

Penzeys is my favorite for herbs and spices that I don't grow in my own garden. Rapid turnover, wide selection, good quality products, delivery to my front door, and reasonable prices are the reasons I like to order from them.

www.penzeys.com

King Arthur

The King Arthur Baker's Catalogue is a very good source of not only flour, but also spices and other conventional and hard-to-find baking ingredients.

www.kingarthurflour.com

INDEX